SPAIN
Attacking Sessions

140 Practices from Goal Analysis of the Spanish National Team

WRITTEN BY MICHAIL TSOKAKTSIDIS

PUBLISHED BY

SPAIN
Attacking Sessions

140 Practices from Goal Analysis of the Spanish National Team

First Published February 2014 by SoccerTutor.com

Info@soccertutor.com | www.SoccerTutor.com

UK: 0208 1234 007 | **US:** (305) 767 4443 | **ROTW:** +44 208 1234 007
ISBN: 978-0-9576705-5-6

Author
Michail Tsokaktsidis © 2014

Edited by
Alex Fitzgerald - SoccerTutor.com

Cover Design by
Alex Macrides, Think Out Of The Box Ltd.
Email: design@thinkootb.com Tel: +44 (0) 208 144 3550

Diagrams
Diagram designs by SoccerTutor.com. All the diagrams in this book have been created using SoccerTutor.com Tactics Manager Software available from **www.SoccerTutor.com**

Note: While every effort has been made to ensure the technical accuracy of the content of this book, neither the author nor publishers can accept any responsibility for any injury or loss sustained as a result of the use of this material.

Meet the Author

MICHAIL TSOKAKTSIDIS

m.tsokaktsidis@gmail.com

- UEFA 'A' Coaching licence

- Bachelor Degree in Physical & Sports Education (specialising in Soccer Conditioning).

I am 38 years old and started playing football at the age of 10 for F.C Doxa Dramas in Greece. I played in all the age levels before progressing to the first team when I was 19 years old. I played for 10 years as a professional at all levels of Greek football for the following teams: Doxa Dramas, Iltex Likoi (WOLVES), Agrotikos Asteras, Ethnikos K., Pandramaikos and Olimpiakos Volou.

During my career I won 6 championships with 5 different teams. At the age of 29 I stopped playing and completed my studies in fitness conditioning and football coaching. I was also a student of the UEFA coaching schools (H.F.F in Greece) and I am a fully certified UEFA A' licence coach.

I started my coaching career in youth football for 3 years and for the last 4 years I have been a head coach in 3 different semi-professional teams in Greece (winning 2 championships). The aim is to develop young players to be professional footballers. My desire is to work at a higher level elsewhere in Europe.

Football is my main focus in life and I have a deep passion for coaching. From very early I was interested in studying training methods as well as to observe and analyse how they are successfully applied (in all phases of the game). I love to learn from the great and successful teams who help to evolve the game.

For my second book of the series, I wanted to use my skills to create great content for coaches all over the world to improve their training sessions. I decided to analyse the most successful national team in recent years, Spain.

They are a team which play attractive, but also effective football and have conquered all before them. The period in which all these goals were scored was 2008-2012 (official competitive games) when Spain won Euro 2008, the World Cup 2010 and Euro 2012.

I think this is a book which provides content that has not been produced before. We have combined a comprehensive analysis of the phases of play which lead to goals with training exercises that can be used for coaches to train the same tactical situations used with many formations such as the 4-4-2, 4-3-3, 4-1-4-1 and 4-2-3-1.

1. We analyse Spain's tactics and the phases of play which lead to their best goals and work on how to recognise and find solutions against different opposition's formations and various tactical situations.

2. We created specific practices to train how to apply the same objectives to your team and achieve the same results.

In life, I believe it is not what you own that matters, but what you create. So I have decided to make this series of books. My favourite motto is 'You can always do much more.'

Contents

CHAPTER 1

Attacking Against Teams which Defend in the Low Zone. 23

CHAPTER 3

Attacking Against Teams which Defend in the High Zone **138**

CHAPTER 4

The Transition from Defence to Attack in the Low Zone **154**

CHAPTER 5

The Transition from Defence to Attack in the Middle Zone **199**

CHAPTER 6

The Transition from Defence to Attack in the High Zone **241**

SUMMARY OF SPAIN BETWEEN 2008 & 2012

The Spanish national team from 2008 to 2012 played in 37 official matches (not including friendly matches) including Euro 2008 in Austria Switzerland, the qualifiers and the World Cup in South Africa in 2010, the qualifiers and the finals of uro 2012 in Poland and Ukraine.

During this period Spain had 2 coaches; Luis Aragones and Vicente Del Bosque.

Luis Aragones won the European Championships in 2008 before Vicente Del Bosque took over on the 15th of July. Spain have since won the World Cup in South Africa (2010) and the European Championships in Poland/Ukraine (2012).

During these 37 matches Spain scored a total of 86 goals (average 2.32 goal per game) and conceded only 16 goals (average 0.43 goal per game).

They **scored in 34 out of the 37 matches** and only failed to score in 3 matches. The first was against Italy (0-0) when Spain won 4-2 on penalties in the quarter final of Euro 2008. The second was against Switzerland (0-1) in the World Cup and the third was against Portugal (0-0) when Spain won 4-2 on penalties in the semi final of Euro 2012.

Spain kept a **clean sheet in 23 of these 37 matches and only twice conceded 2 goals in one match**. The first was away against Bosnia Herzegovina in a World Cup qualifier (won 2-5) and the second was away against Scotland in a qualifying match for Euro 2012 (won 2-3).

The numbers do not always tell the whole truth, but in this case I think they speak for themselves and show us that during this

period, the Spanish national team were not only very strong in the attacking phase but also very strong across all 4 phases of the game.

What is very important is how Spain created these goals and how they found solutions in different game situations and against different defensive organisation.

49 of Spain's 86 goals were scored against opponents who used an organised defence.

37 goals were scored against opponents who defended in the low zone, 10 goals against opponents who defended in the middle zone and only 2 goals were scored against opponents who defended in the high zone.

22 of Spain's 86 goals were scored in the transition from defence to attack. 8 goals were made in the transition to attack from the low zone, 8 from the middle zone and 6 from the high zone.

And finally, 15 of Spain's 86 goals were scored from set plays; 3 from corner kicks, 6 from free kicks and 6 from penalties.

Spain's Goal Statistics 2008-2012

	Number of Goals (37 Matches)	Percentage
Total Goals Scored	86 (2.32 per game)	-
Transition to Attack from the Low Zone	8	9.3%
Transition to Attack from the Middle Zone	8	9.3%
Transition to Attack from the High Zone	6	7%
The Opposition Defending in the Low Zone	37	43%
The Opposition Defending in the Middle Zone	10	11.6%
The Opposition Defending in the High Zone	2	2.3%
Set Plays (Total)	15	17.5%
Free Kicks	6	7%
Corner Kicks	3	3.5%
Penalties	6	7%

UEFA EURO 2008 FINALS

Spain started their dominance in European and World football in Euro 2008 with Luis Aragones as their coach. In their 6 matches at the tournament they scored 12 goals (2 per game). Only in their match against Italy did they fail to score.

Spain scored 7 goals against organised defences but only 3 when the opposition defended in the low zone. They scored 4 goals in the transition phase (3 from the low zone and 1 from the middle zone). Finally, they scored 1 goal from a set play (corner kick).

This shows clearly that in this tournament Spain were beginning their building up from the back style of play which we saw more of later and still see today. It also shows that the opposition tried to play against Spain differently to how they do now, I.e. not just passive play or deep defending in their own half, but playing more defence in the middle and in some cases in the high zone of the pitch.

Spain's Goal Statistics During the UEFA Euro 2008 Finals

	Number of Goals (6 Matches)	Percentage
Total Goals Scored	12 (2 per game)	-
Transition to Attack from the Low Zone	3	25%
Transition to Attack from the Middle Zone	1	8%
Transition to Attack from the High Zone	-	-
The Opposition Defending in the Low Zone	3	25%
The Opposition Defending in the Middle Zone	3	25%
The Opposition Defending in the High Zone	1	8%
Set Plays (Total)	1	8%
Free Kicks	-	-
Corner Kicks	1	7%
Penalties	-	-

SPAIN Attacking Sessions

Spain Formation (4-4-2) & Players For Uefa Euro 2008 Finals

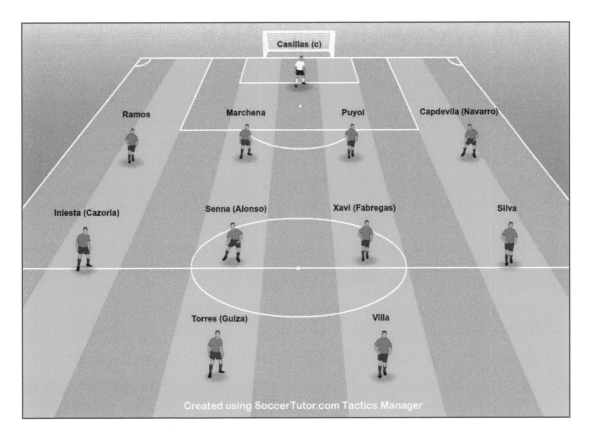

[In the final against Germany, Spain used a 4-1-4-1 because Villa was injured. Silva and Iniesta played as wide forwards and Fabregas played in behind Torres.]

When attacking, Spain were set up in the 4-4-2 formation shown in the diagram.

Silva and Iniesta played as wide midfielders, but much of their play when Spain were in possession was further inside as they often moved into central positions to create a numerical superiority in there. This often created space for the full backs (Capdevila and Ramos) to attack in advanced areas on the flank.

With the wide midfielders playing much of their game inside, this also meant either Torres or Villa would exploit the space on the flank. They would often make runs into wide positions, which would stretch the defensive line and create more space in the penalty area for midfield runners.

The striker who dropped off the most (and made runs high up on the left flank) was Villa who felt most comfortable in these areas.

QUALIFICATION FOR FIFA WORLD CUP 2010

After the big victory in 2008 a new era started with Pep Guardiola building his own empire at Barcelona which brought its own tactical revolution, playing the most attractive and efficient football in history. This heavily influenced the playing style of the Spanish national team. The managerial reins were now passed to Vicente Del Bosque and they had many players from Barcelona.

During the 2010 qualification campaign, Spain scored 28 goals in 10 matches (average 2.8 per game).In these 10 matches, Spain scored in every game and also kept 6 clean sheets. They conceded only 5 goals (average 0.5 per game).

The most goals (9) came from the opposition defending in the low zone, 2 in the middle zone and 1 in the high zone.

The transition phase from defence to attack was a very strong feature for Spain in this period also. They scored a total of 9 goals this way; 2 in the transition to attack from the low zone, 4 from the middle zone and 3 from the transition to attack in the high zone.

The scoring was completed with 7 goals from set plays (4 free kicks and 3 penalties).

Spain's Goal Statistics During the FIFA World Cup Qualifying Campaign

	Number of Goals (10 Matches)	Percentage
Total Goals Scored	28 (2.8 per game)	-
Transition to Attack from the Low Zone	2	7.1%
Transition to Attack from the Middle Zone	4	14.2%
Transition to Attack from the High Zone	3	10.7%
The Opposition Defending in the Low Zone	9	32.1%
The Opposition Defending in the Middle Zone	2	7.1%
The Opposition Defending in the High Zone	1	3.5%
Set Plays (Total)	7	25%
Free Kicks	4	14.3%
Corner Kicks	-	-
Penalties	3	10.7%

SPAIN Attacking Sessions

FIFA WORLD CUP FINALS 2010

The tournament which established Spain as the greatest football power in recent years was the 2010 World Cup in South Africa. Although they started with a defeat in against Switzerland (0-1), they responded with very mature performances and step by step, they proved themselves to be the best team in the world.

They played 7 matches, scoring in 6 of them (a total of 8 goals, averaging 1.14 per game) and keeping clean sheets in 5 of their matches (all 4 knock out matches were won with a 1-0 scoreline).

2 goals were scored when the opposition defended in the low zone, 1 goal against an organised opposition in the middle zone and no goals with the opposition defending in the high zone (mainly because the opponent did not play defensively in this zone).

4 goals were scored in the transition from defence to attack, 3 of which were in the transition to attack from the low zone and 1 was in the transition to attack from the middle zone.

Finally, 1 goal was scored from a set play with a corner kick in a victory in the semi final against Germany (1-0).

Spain's Goal Statistics During the FIFA World Cup Finals 2010

	Number of Goals (7 Matches)	Percentage
Total Goals Scored	8 (1.14 per game)	-
Transition to Attack from the Low Zone	3	25%
Transition to Attack from the Middle Zone	1	12.5%
Transition to Attack from the High Zone	-	-
The Opposition Defending in the Low Zone	2	37.5%
The Opposition Defending in the Middle Zone	1	12.5%
The Opposition Defending in the High Zone	-	-
Set Plays (Total)	1	12.5%
Free Kicks	-	-
Corner Kicks	1	12.5%
Penalties	-	-

SPAIN FORMATION (4-3-3) & PLAYERS FOR FIFA WORLD CUP FINALS 2010

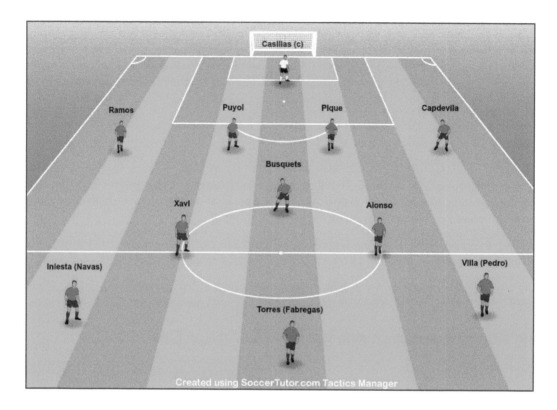

During this tournament, Busquets became very important to Spain's system. His ability to screen the defence and use his positioning to win the ball or maintain possession were key. The Barcelona style of play under Pep Guardiola had started to really impact the Spanish national side.

Xavi was then able to dominate other teams with his great passing. In the final, Xavi completed more passes than any other player, ran further than any other player and dictated the game from the centre of midfield.

When Navas played, he would often beat the defender on the outside and cross from the byline The full backs also provided the width in this formation. This was important as teams had started to play much deeper against Spain and it was harder to attack through the centre.

Iniesta played most of his game inside to help Spain create a 4v3 numerical superiority in centre midfield to either win the ball back quickly or maintain possession. When the other team were in possession, Spain would press their centre midfielders to deny them time and space on the ball, preventing them being able to play killer passes.

There were slight modifications to Spain's formation throughout the 7 games in the tournament as they also used the 4-2-3-1, the 4-3-2-1 and the 4-1-3-2 (against Paraguay in the quarter final).

QUALIFICATION FOR UEFA EURO 2012

Champions of Europe in 2008 and champions of the World in 2010, Spain were now at their finest. With a Barcelona playing style at its zenith, the qualification of Euro 2012 was their most productive.

In just 8 matches (scoring in all matches) they scored 26 goals (3.25 per game). The domination of their opponents was now bigger than ever and the majority of the teams tried to defend in their own half of the pitch and in mostly within the low zone.

17 of Spain's 26 goals were scored against opponents who defended in the low zone, only 2 in the middle zone and none against teams who defended in the high zone (mainly because the opponent did not defend against Spain in this zone).

There were also 3 goals from transition phase; 1 from the transition to attack from the middle zone and 2 from the transition to attack from the high zone.

Finally, they scored 4 goals from set plays (2 from free kicks and 2 from penalties).

Spain's Goal Statistics During the UEFA Euro 2012 Qualifying Campaign

	Number of Goals (8 Matches)	Percentage
Total Goals Scored	26 (3.25 per game)	-
Transition to Attack from the Low Zone	-	-
Transition to Attack from the Middle Zone	1	3.35%
Transition to Attack from the High Zone	2	7.7%
The Opposition Defending in the Low Zone	17	65.3%
The Opposition Defending in the Middle Zone	2	7.7%
The Opposition Defending in the High Zone	-	-
Set Plays (Total)	4	15.4%
Free Kicks	2	7.7%
Corner Kicks	-	-
Penalties	2	7.7%

UEFA EURO 2012 FINALS

In this competition, Spain confirmed their superiority and established themselves as the most successful national team in recent years scoring (in all matches again) 12 goals in 6 matches (2 per game). 5 goals were scored against opponents who defended in the low zone and 3 goals against opponents who defended in the middle zone.

Spain did not score any goals against opponents who defended in the high zone (again this is because teams did not defend against Spain in this zone).

2 goals came from the transition phase, with 1 goal when Spain won the ball in the middle zone and went from defence to attack and 1 from the transition to attack from the high zone.

Spain also scored 2 goals from set plays (1 corner kick and 1 penalty).

Spain's Goal Statistics During the UEFA Euro 2012 Finals

	Number of Goals (6 Matches)	Percentage
Total Goals Scored	12 (2 per game)	-
Transition to Attack from the Low Zone	-	-
Transition to Attack from the Middle Zone	1	8.3%
Transition to Attack from the High Zone	1	8.3%
The Opposition Defending in the Low Zone	6	50%
The Opposition Defending in the Middle Zone	2	16.6%
The Opposition Defending in the High Zone	-	-
Set Plays (Total)	2	16.6%
Free Kicks	-	-
Corner Kicks	1	8.3%
Penalties	1	8.3%

SPAIN FORMATION (4-2-3-1) & PLAYERS FOR UEFA EURO 2012 FINALS

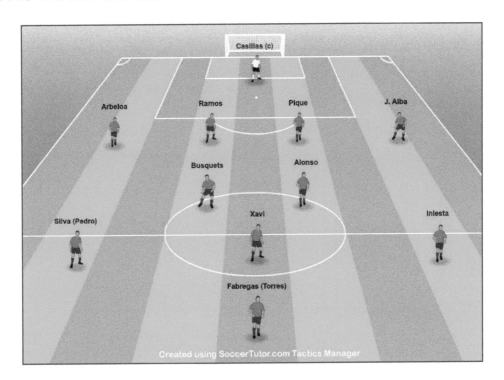

With this 4-3-3 formation during the Euro 2012 tournament, Spain played mainly through the centre (the full backs provided the width). Teams were very negative against them and Spain scored few goals in their first 5 games, although they only conceded 1 goal (against Italy) because they had so much good possession of the ball.

Spain used constant, quick, short passes in midfield with a numerical advantage. As the wide forwards/midfielders would often play inside, Spain would have 6 players in the centre of the pitch (including Fabregas who played as a striker) and the full backs provided the width. After keeping the ball in the centre, the first pass in behind the defensive line would often be to a full back on the flank (especially to J. Alba).

The Final vs Italy (4-0)

Everything changed in the final against Italy when Spain had by far their best performance of the tournament. Spain still attacked mainly through the centre, but were much more successful.

J. Alba had a fantastic tournament and played particularly well in the final. He made many forward runs to join the attack and scored the second goal with a run from deep in between the 2 centre backs.

The 3rd goal which we analyse later was also scored with a pass in between the 2 Italian centre backs for Torres.

Coaching Format

1. Goal Analysis.
2. Full Training Session from Goal Analysis.
    *   Technical / Functional Unopposed Practices
    *   Tactical Opposed Practices
    *   Rules, Progressions, Variations & Coaching Points (if applicable)

Key

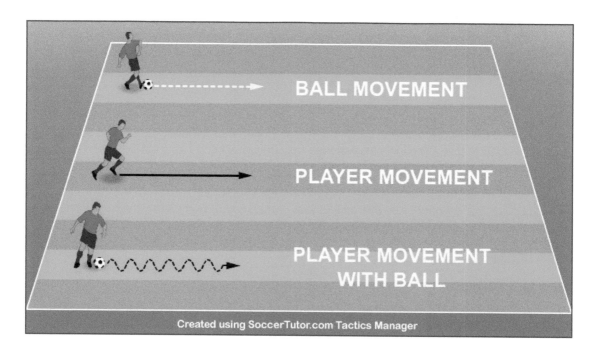

CHAPTER 1

Attacking Against Teams which Defend in the Low Zone

Attacking Against Teams which Defend in the Low Zone

Spain scored 37 of their 86 goals (mostly from 2009-12) in this period against opponents who defended in the low zone. In these situations the opposition would have many players in the low zone (minimum 8) and all of them would be behind the ball.

In this situation Spain would score in 5 different ways:

1. Attacking Inside the Penalty Area

In this situation Spain have pushed the opposition back into their own penalty area and attack with many players in and around the penalty area. The ball is played into the box with good passing or dribbling from one player. The player who receives a pass inside the box works with high quality and speed (under pressure of time and space) to finish the attack.

2. Attacking in and Around the Penalty Area *(combination play or passing in behind the defensive line)*

In this situation the opposition also have many players on the edge of the box and Spain found solutions in 2 different ways.

1. Maintain possession and at the correct time use quick combination play on the edge of the box (usually between 3 players) that usually included different variations of a third man run.

2. The second way was to eliminate the 2 lines of the opposition (midfield and defence) with a technical pass in behind the defensive line into an area where another player has moved into space (exploiting this to finish the attack).

3. Shooting from Outside of the Penalty Area

The Spanish team would work very well to maintain possession in the opposition half and then create a situation for one player to be in a good position near the penalty area in the centre. This player then shoots from outside the box, finishing the attack.

4. Attacking from the Flanks

When the opposition had many players in the centre of the pitch, Spain would use the full width of the pitch. They would often switch play from side to side to change the point of attack and exploit the weak side of the opposition.

In this case, depending on the opposition they were playing, Spain would use crosses with a mid-height (1) or low crosses (2).

When crosses with a mid-height were used, the opposition were positioned on the edge of the penalty area and the cross would go in behind the defensive line (mostly to the far post).

When using low crosses Spain would first create a numerical superiority (2v1) on the flank with an overlapping (or under-lapping) movement and the cross could go to either the near or fat post.

5. 1v1 / 2v2 Play (individual creativity)

Finally we show Spain's creativity where one player has the ball in a 1v1 or 1v2 situation. The player/s used their technical quality and speed to exploit the opposition and finish the attack.

GOAL ANALYSIS

Attacking Inside the Penalty Area (1)

10-Sep-2008: World Cup 2010 Qualifying

Spain 4-0 Armenia (1st Goal): Capdevila - Assist: Iniesta

Spain in a 4-4-2 vs Armenia in a 4-2-3-1

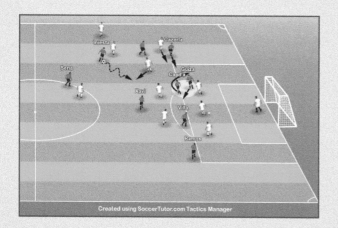

The opposition have 9 players behind the ball. Spain have 5 players between the midfield line and the defensive line.

Iniesta dribbles inside from the left to try and draw an opponent out of position to cause imbalance.

The players in front of him check away from their markers (Guiza & Capdevila swap positions) to create space and provide Iniesta with support and passing options.

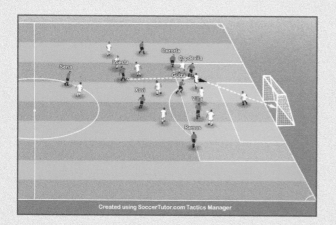

At the correct time, Iniesta passes forward to Capdevila inside the penalty area where we have a 5v4 situation in a limited space.

Capdevila takes an excellent directional first touch and with his second touch, scores the goal under pressure from a defender.

GOAL ANALYSIS

Attacking Inside the Penalty Area (2)

10-Sep-2008: World Cup 2010 Qualifying

Spain 4-0 Armenia (2nd Goal): Villa - Assist: Iniesta

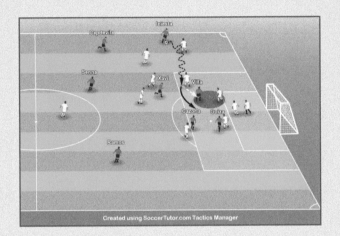

We have the same situation again with 9 outfield players within 25 yards from the goal. Iniesta has the ball on the left, Capdevila provides support with Senna and Ramos providing defensive balance.

There are 3 (+1) Spanish players inside the box and Iniesta shows good creativity to win the 1v1 situation.

When the second defender (cover) goes up to him, he passes to Villa and continues to run into the penalty area.

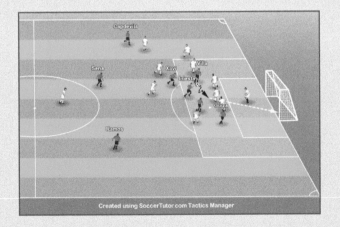

With Villa in possession, we now have a 4 (+1) v 5 situation inside the penalty area.

Villa controls the ball quickly and moves it onto his right foot. He finishes with the inside of his foot into the opposite corner of the net.

GOAL ANALYSIS

Attacking Inside the Penalty Area (3)

10-Sep-2008: World Cup 2010 Qualifying

Spain 4-0 Armenia (3rd Goal): Villa - Assist: Alonso

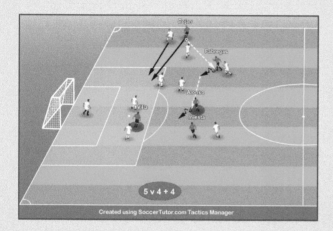

The opposition have 4 (+4) players at the back and Spain attack with 5 players (2 attackers, 2 centre midfielders and a left midfielder).

Bojan passes from the right inside to Fabregas and then makes a diagonal run into the penalty area. Bojan asks for the ball in the most dangerous area for the opponent. This gives Fabregas support in front and another forward passing option.

Fabregas dribbles forward up to the opponent and then passes to Alonso who is free in the centre.

Alonso also dribbles forward.

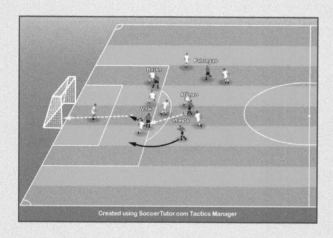

When the centre back closes down Alonso, he passes the ball to Villa who has taken up a very good position in the penalty area.

Villa (positioned inside the right back) receives on the half turn, shielding the ball from the right back with good body shape.

He finishes well past the goalkeeper.

The same situation occurred against Scotland:

12-Oct-2010: European Championship 2012 Qualifying

Scotland 2-3 Spain (2nd Goal): Iniesta

GOAL ANALYSIS

Attacking Inside the Penalty Area (4)

06-Sep-2011: European Championship 2012 Qualifying

Spain 6-0 Liechtenstein (5th Goal): Villa - Assist: Mata

Spain in a 4-3-3 vs Liechtenstein in a 4-2-3-1

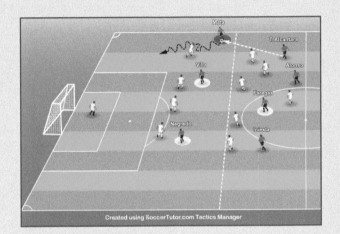

Alcantara with one pass to the right flank (to Mata) puts the opposition's 4 midfielders and 2 attackers behind the ball.

For the moment we have a 3v4 situation.

Mata has more quality and is faster than the left back and shows good creativity to win the 1v1 on the right flank.

Mata beats the opponent and dribbles with quality and high speed into the box, and now we have a 3v3 (+ upcoming players).

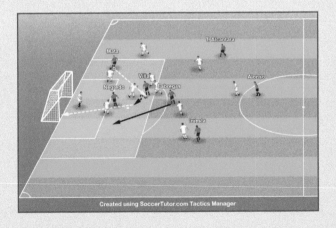

The centre back closes Mata down and he passes back to Villa just inside the penalty area.

The other attacker's (Negredo) run takes the right back with him.

Villa is up against the other centre back and takes a good directional first touch to the left, showing quality technique to shoot and score the 5th goal for Spain.

SESSION FOR THIS TOPIC *(7 Practices)*

1. Directional First Touch Continuous Finishing Practice

PART 1

PART 2

Objective

To develop the correct body shape, a quality first touch and finishing inside the penalty area.

Description

In an area 25 x 25 yards we work with 5 players and 2 goalkeepers. We have 2 full sized goals and 5 mannequins in the positions shown in the diagram. 1 player works inside and the other 4 have a ball and stay on the outside.

The inside player starts the practice from the left or right of the first mannequin and runs in slalom between them. Player 1 passes the ball to him, he takes a good and quick directional first touch with the left foot and shoots at goal.

He immediately moves to receive the next pass from player 2. This time the first touch must be a turn in the direction of the other goal (as shown in the diagram) before shooting again.

As shown in diagram 2, the inside player now runs round the end mannequin (changing direction) and receives the next pass from player 3, takes a quality and quick first touch with the right foot before shooting in the goal at the top again.

He then receives the next pass from player 4 (between the mannequins), takes a directional first touch towards the other goal and finishes with the last shot.

When the sequence is completed and the player has taken all 4 shots, he switches roles with one of the outside players. Any other player from outside can then restart the practice. Each player must start the practice from both sides (minimum 2 repetitions inside for each player).

Rule

At the beginning the player has a maximum of 3 touches to shoot. Progress to 2 touches.

Coaching Points

Monitor these aspects for this practice:

1. The correct body shape when receiving a pass; opening up and receiving on the half turn with the back foot.
2. The weight of the first touch so it is out of the feet and towards goal, but still close enough as to not lose possession or shooting chance in a real game situation.
3. The proper technique for shooting at goal (focus on accuracy of finishing and not power).

PROGRESSION
2. Directional First Touch Continuous Finishing Practice (2)

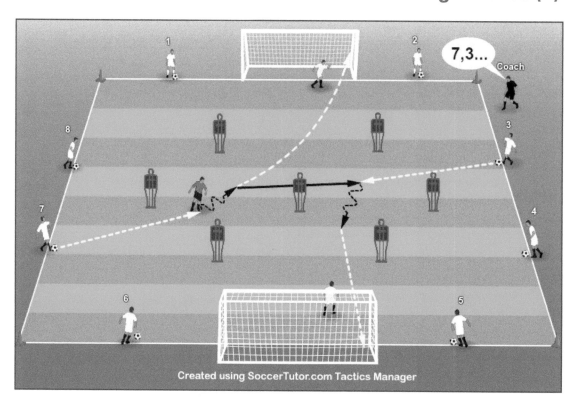

Created using SoccerTutor.com Tactics Manager

Objective

To develop the correct body shape, a quality directional first touch and finishing.

Description

For this progression we add an extra 4 outside players so we have 8 in total. We also add 2 mannequins and position the 8 as shown in the diagram. Each player has a number and waits for the coach to call it out.

The coach calls out a number and the inside player must recognise where that outside player is very quickly and move into the correct position to receive, take the ball with a quick directional first touch and shoot in either of the 2 goals.

The inside player shoots with all 8 balls and then switches roles with an outside player.

Progression

Put the outside numbered players in random positions (not numerical order).

Coaching Points

1. In this exercise we must pay attention to the pace and intensity. We do not want to work power speed, but rather quick and quality perception, decision making and execution of movement.
2. The inside player needs good anticipation and quick reactions to get into the right positions.

34

PROGRESSION - VARIATION
3. Directional First Touch and Finishing Inside the Penalty Area

Created using SoccerTutor.com Tactics Manager

Objective
To develop the correct body shape, a quality directional first touch and finishing inside the penalty area.

Description
In this practice we adapt the previous drill and use half a full pitch. One player works within the penalty area where there are 7 mannequins as shown in the diagram. We have 5 numbered players in the positions shown, all outside of the box.

The coach calls out a number and the player must receive a pass from that player and take a quality first touch before shooting with the second touch.

The inside player shoots with all 5 balls and then switches roles with an outside player.

Coaching Point
The accuracy and weight of the pass is very important, so the player inside the penalty area is able to take a directional first touch and finish quickly.

PROGRESSION
4. Quick Finishing in a 6 v 6 (+8) Small Sided Game

Created using SoccerTutor.com Tactics Manager

Objective
We work on the correct body shape, quality directional first touches and finishing in a small sided game.

Description
In an area 25 x 25 yards we have a 6v6 small sided game (+ 8 neutral players on the outside). The game starts with one team or the coach can pass a ball into play.

The neutrals play with the team in possession creating a 13v5 situation for the outfield players. This huge advantage should make it easier to create space and shoot quickly.

The objective for both teams when they have possession is to shoot within a certain time limit or within a number of touches of the ball. This should depend on the age group or level of the players.

Rules
1. The attack must finish within 6, 8 or 10 seconds / The attack must finish within 6, 8 or 10 touches (team).
2. All players have unlimited touches (or 2-3 touches) and neutrals have 1 touch.

Coaching Point
The teams should look to create a numerical superiority around the ball zone, so they are more able to create space quickly for a final pass, directional first touch and shot.

PROGRESSION
5. Quick Finishing in a 6 v 6 Small Sided Game

Description

All the objectives and rules are exactly the same as the previous practice, but we have removed the 8 neutral players and play a 6v6 small sided game.

The players now have to be much sharper to create space and must try to get their shots off extremely quickly.

Coaching Points

1. Players should take any chance they get to take a good touch to create half a yard of space and shoot.
2. The correct body shape should be monitored (opening up) and receiving/passing with the back foot (foot furthest away from the ball).
3. Players should vary their passes - passes to feet and passes into space.

PROGRESSION
6. Quick Finishing in a 2 Zone 6 v 6 (+4) Small Sided Game

Created using SoccerTutor.com Tactics Manager

Description

In an area 30 x 20 yards we divide the pitch into 2 zones. We play a 6v6 small sided game (+4 neutrals players at the sides). In the defensive half we have a 2v3 situation and in the attacking half we have a 3v2.

The game starts with a goalkeeper and the team in possession must find solutions to score (under pressure of time and space) using the neutral players and the 3 attacking players. All players must stay within their zones at all times.

When an attack is finished or the ball goes out of play, the game starts again from the other goalkeeper.

Different Rules

1. Teams have 6-10 seconds to finish their attack.
2. The team can use a maximum of 10 touches (team) to finish their attack.
3. All players have unlimited touches and the neutrals have 1 touch.
4. The defenders in each zone are limited to 2 touches, attackers have 3 touches and the neutrals have 1 touch.

Coaching Point

Teams should use the wide neutral players to create a numerical superiority and space to shoot quickly.

PROGRESSION

7. Directional First Touch and Quick Finishing in a Position Specific Zonal Game

Description

For the final practice in this session we use an area double the size of the penalty area split into 2 zones. We play an 11v11 game. Each team has 4 players in each grid and 2 additional players outside of the attacking half.

The red team use a 4-4-2 formation. The 4 defenders are in the defensive half, the left midfielder (8) and right midfielder (7) are at the sides and the 2 centre midfielders (6 & 10) + 2 attackers (11 & 9) are in the attacking half.

The white team use a 4-3-3. They have 4 defenders in the defensive half, the left forward (11) and the right forward (7) are at the sides, the centre midfielder (6), 2 attacking midfielders (8 & 10) and the striker (9) are inside the attacking half.

The teams play a normal game, except the players are not allowed to leave their zone. The side players are not allowed to shoot or pass to each other unless they enter the attacking zone with the ball (as shown in diagram).

Different Rules

1. All players have unlimited touches.
2. Limit the defenders to 2-3 touches, but the attackers still have unlimited touches.
3. All players are limited to 3 touches.
4. The defenders and side players are limited to 3 touches and the attackers/neutrals have 2 touches.

Coaching Point

The focus of this game is to pass the ball to the players inside the penalty area who should take good directional touches and shoot quickly (including dribbling up to opponents and passing to a free teammate).

GOAL ANALYSIS

Attacking in and Around the Penalty Area (1)

06-Sep-2011: European Championship 2012 Qualifying

Spain 3-0 Russia (2nd Goal): Guiza - Assist: Fabregas

Spain in a 4-4-2 vs Russia in a 4-1-3-2

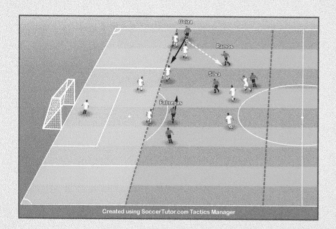

Guiza (like Bojan for the third goal against Armenia) has the opposition's left back in front of him and passes to Ramos inside and then makes a diagonal run into the penalty area.

Russia have the 4-1-3 part of their formation in the defensive half.

Fabregas moves to the right and provides support to Ramos.

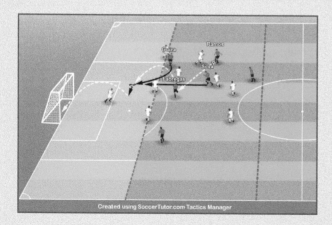

Ramos is under pressure from the defensive midfielder and the centre back.

Ramos passes to Fabregas and while the ball is travelling, Guiza and Silva make third man runs into the penalty area.

Fabregas plays a technical chipped 1 touch pass in behind the defensive line (in between the left back and right centre back).

Guiza gets there ahead of the left back and controls with his chest. He executes a chipped shot over the goalkeeper to score.

40

GOAL ANALYSIS
Attacking in and Around the Penalty Area (2)
29-Mar-2011: European Championship 2012 Qualifying
Lithuania 1-3 Spain (3rd Goal): Mata - Assist: Silva
Spain in a 4-3-3 vs Lithuania in a 4-4-2

Alonso is under pressure from the right midfielder on the flank and passes to Xavi. Xavi has the 2 Lithuanian strikers left and right of him and the other 7 opposition players in front of him.

There are 5 Spanish players in behind the opposition's midfield line and level with the defensive line.

Silva drops off at a good angle to support Xavi.

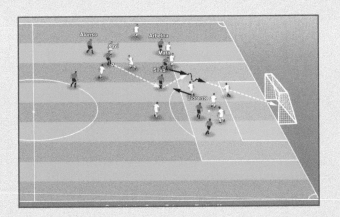

Xavi passes to Silva and while the ball is travelling, Mata makes a third man run into the penalty area.

Silva plays a 1 touch pass into Mata's path.

Mata shows good control and finishes well past the rushing goalkeeper.

SESSION FOR THIS TOPIC *(6 Practices)*

1. One Touch Combination Play and 3rd Man Run

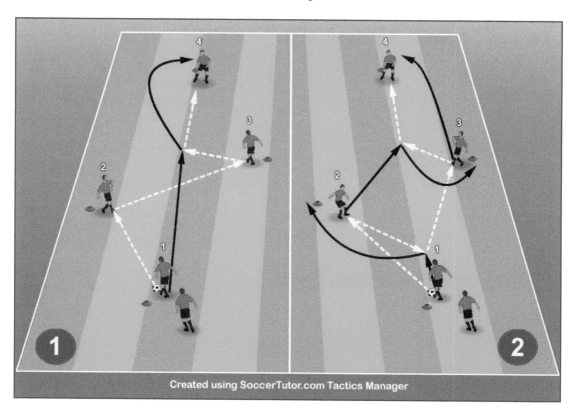

Created using SoccerTutor.com Tactics Manager

Objective

We work on our passing, timing and movement in one touch combinations, with the focus on 3rd man runs.

Description

1. We have 6 players and use 4 cones (in the positions shown). Player 1 starts with 1 ball and passes to player 2 who passes to Player 3. As soon as Player 1 has played his pass, he moves forward (3rd man run) and receives the next pass from Player 3 and passes to Player 4 using 1 touch.

    The practice continues from player 4 now as he passes to player 3. Players 2 and 3 stay in their positions until the coach changes them.

2. Player 1 plays a one-two combination with Player 2. Player 1 passes to player 3. As soon as Player 2 has played his pass, he moves across (3rd man run) to receive the next pass from Player 3 and passes to Player 4 using 1 touch. All players now move up one position (1 to 2, 2 to 3, 3 to 4). Now the practice continues from this side.

    Both drills must be executed from both sides.

PROGRESSION
2. One Touch Combination Play and 3rd Man Run with Finishing

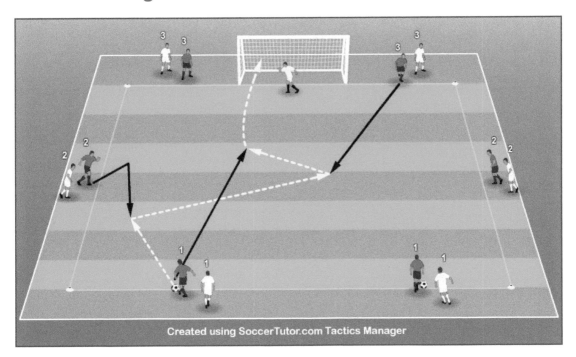

Created using SoccerTutor.com Tactics Manager

Objective
We have the same objectives as the previous practice, but we also now work on finishing.

Description
In an area 30 x 30 yards we work with 12 players and a goalkeeper. We have 6 positions with 2 players on each one. We have 2 groups and each group has 3 positions (numbered) with 6 players.

Player 1 passes to player 2 who checks away from the cone before receiving. Player 2 passes to Player 3 who has run deep to receive.

As soon as Player 1 has played his pass, he moves forward towards goal (third man run) and receives the first time pass from Player 3 and shoots at goal.

Each player in the first group move up one position (1 to 2, 2 to 3, 3 to 1). The drill continues with the second group. Player 1 on the right starts the same sequence.

Coaching Points
1. The players need to use the correct angles and body shape to be able to make the right passes.
2. Player 2's first movement should be the same as if checking away from a marker before moving to receive.

VARIATION

3. One Touch Combination Play and 3rd Man Run with Finishing (2)

Created using SoccerTutor.com Tactics Manager

Description

In this variation, all that changes is the sequence of the passes and the movements.

Player 1 passes to player 2 who passes back to player 1. Player 1 then passes to player 3 who has run deep to receive.

As soon as Player 2 has played his pass, he moves diagonally towards goal (3rd man run) and receives the first time pass from Player 3 and shoots at goal.

PROGRESSION
4. Attacking Combination Play with 3rd Man Runs in a 6 v 6 (+2) Small Sided Game

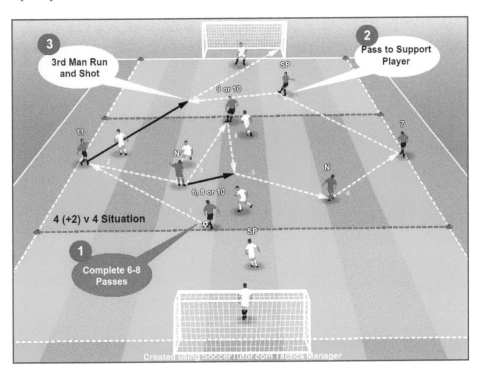

Objective

To develop quick combination play, 3rd man runs and finishing in a small sided game.

Description

In an area 38 x 14 yards divide the pitch into 3 zones. The middle zone is 14 x 14 yards and the 2 end zones are both 12 x 14 yards each. In the middle zone we have a 4v4 and 2 neutral players. Each team has 1 extra support player in the high zone.

The game starts with one team in possession in the middle zone with a 4 (+2) v 4 situation. In this example the reds are in possession and the 4 red players can only move along the sides of the middle zone. The 2 neutral players move around inside and provide support for them.

The objective for the team in possession is to complete 6-8 passes and then pass to their support player in the high zone. If this happens, another player (using a 3rd man run) runs forward to support, receives a first time pass from the support player and shoots at goal.

The support players can stay the same or can change position with the player who shoots.

Rules

1. Red and white players are limited to 2 touches in the middle zone and 1 touch in the end zones.
2. Neutral players and support players are limited to 1 touch.

PROGRESSION

5. Attacking Combination Play with 3rd Man Runs in an 8 v 8 (+2) Small Sided Game

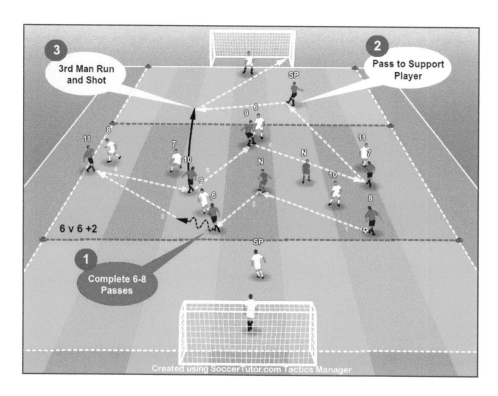

Description

We divide the pitch into 3 zones as shown. Both end zones are 16 yards in length. In the middle zone we have a 6v6 and 2 neutral players. Each team has 1 extra support player in the high zone. The red team in are in a 3-3 formation (from 4-3-3) and the whites are in a 4-2 (from 4-4-2).

The objective for the team in possession is to enter the final zone. To do this they must play a forward pass to the support player, with another middle zone player making a 3rd man run to receive in behind and shoot.

The support players can stay the same or can change position with the player who shoots.

Rules

1. All players in the middle zone have unlimited touches (or 3 touches) and the neutrals have 2 touches.
2. The support players are limited to 1 touch.
3. The player who makes the 3rd man run must finish with 1 touch.

PROGRESSION
6. Attacking Combination Play with 3rd Man Runs in a Position Specific 3 Zone Game

8 v 8

Red Team Low Zone

Created using SoccerTutor.com Tactics Manager

Description

We now extend the area to the full width of the pitch. The red team have 8 players in the middle zone and all their players except for the centre backs (4 & 5) make a 2-3-3 formation. The whites have 8 players in the middle zone in a 4-4 formation. In the low zone for the red team we have 2 red centre backs and 2 white attackers (once the ball is played into the middle zone they should all stay within 1-2 yards of the line).

The game always starts with the red goalkeeper and the objective is to enter the final zone. To do this they must use a combination including a player making a 3rd man run to receive the ball in behind the defensive line.

The white team can defend in the final zone as soon as the ball is played in there. If they win the ball they try to score in the opposite goal, but they have limited touches or time to do so (6-8 passes or 8-10 seconds). This rule forces the red team to move quickly from attack to defence (negative transition).

Rules

1. The 2 red centre backs can support in the possession phase, but are not allowed to enter the middle zone.

2. The 2 white attackers only play in transition to attack for the white team (do not defend in possession phase).

3. All red players can return and enter their low zone in the transition to defence phase.

4. All players have unlimited touches except for the red players in the final zone who have 2-3 touches or 4-6 seconds to finish their attack.

5. If the white team score the goal counts double.

47

GOAL ANALYSIS

Attacking in and Around the Penalty Area (3)

07-Oct-2011: European Championship 2012 Qualifying

Czech Republic 0-2 Spain (2nd Goal): Alonso - Assist: Silva

Spain in a 4-3-3 vs Czech Republic in a 4-2-3-1

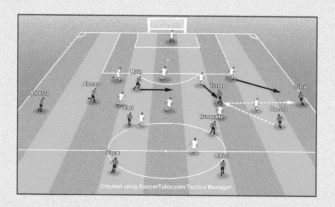

Ramos passes the ball to Torres in behind the Czech midfield.

Torres is put under pressure by the left centre back and passes to Silva on the right flank.

The left back moves out wide to press him and Mata moves across to provide support.

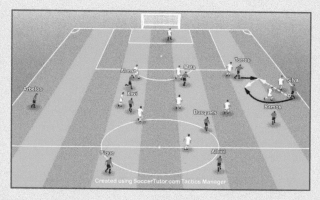

Silva plays an excellent give and go (1-2 combination) with Torres and receives the ball inside, eliminating the left attacking midfielder, the left back and the left centre back from the game.

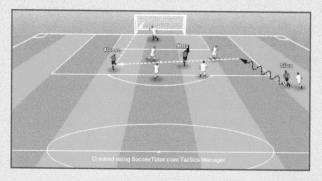

Silva dribbles into the box in a 3 v 2 (+2) situation. Mata moves to the near post and Alonso to the far post.

Silva hits a low cross to Alonso who scores with a 1 touch finish. This was very good cooperation and combination play.

GOAL ANALYSIS

Attacking in and Around the Penalty Area (4)

03-Sep-2010: European Championship 2012 Qualifying

Liechtenstein 0-4 Spain (3rd Goal): Torres - Assist: Silva

Spain in a 4-4-2 vs Liechtenstein in a 4-2-3-1

Spain had a corner kick and the ball was cleared to Alonso. The opposition defence is unbalanced on the right side (bad positions and synchronisation in 2-3-1). Alonso passes into this space to Fabregas.

Spain have a 1v1 with every member of the back 4. Fabregas dribbles inside and creates a numerical advantage (2v1) with Torres against his direct opponent.

Torres checks away from his marker and Fabregas passes into the space.

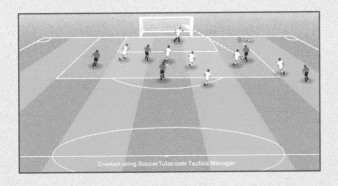

Torres times his run well and gets ahead of the defender.

There are 3 other attackers and 3 Liechtenstein defenders in the penalty area as well.

Torres scores the goal at the near post.

SESSION FOR THIS TOPIC *(4 Practices)*

1. One-Two Combination & Dribbling Practice

A

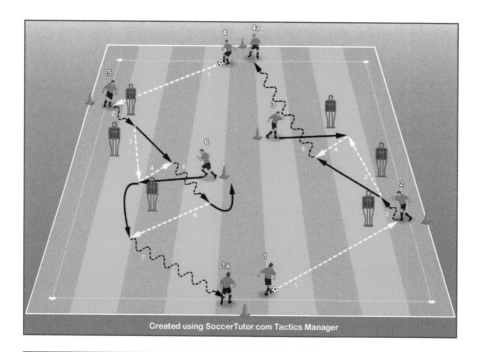

B

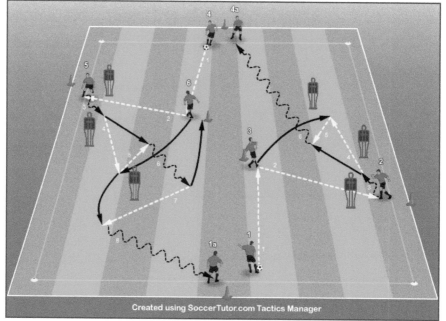

Objective

We work on our attacking combination play with the focus on one-two combinations and dribbling.

Description

A) In an area 40 x 20 yards we have 8 players, 6 mannequins and 4 cones. The players are in the positions shown in the diagram, with 2 players at the start and end positions (with a ball at each end).

The practice starts simultaneously with the 2 players in positions 1 & 4. From the bottom, player 1 passes to player 2 who takes a directional first touch (past the mannequin). Player 3 makes a supporting movement to his left and player 2 plays a 1-2 combination with him. Player 2 then dribbles the ball quickly to position 4.

Simultaneously, player 4 passes to player 5 who takes a directional first touch (past the mannequin). Player 6 makes a supporting movement to his left and player 5 plays a one-two combination with him.

Player 5 dribbles forwards and player 6 runs round the mannequin. Player 5 passes to him into the space and he dribbles back to the start.

B) In the second diagram we have 2 balls again. Player 1 passes to player 3 who passes to player 2. Player 3 makes a diagonal movement (support) for the next pass and player 2 plays a one-two combination with him, then dribbles to position 4.

Simultaneously, player 4 passes forwards to player 6 who passes to player 5. Player 6 makes a diagonal support movement for the next pass and player 6 plays a one-two combination with him. Player 5 dribbles forwards and player 6 runs round the mannequin. Player 5 passes to him into the space and he dribbles back to the start.

Coaching Points

1. This practice should include quick and quality short passes to feet and into space.
2. Players should check away from their stations before moving to receive and providing good angles of support.
3. The one-two combinations need the correct weight and timing of pass which should be in front player to run onto without slowing down.
4. Good awareness and optical/verbal communication is needed.

PROGRESSION
2. One-Two Combination, 3rd Man Run and Finishing Practice

Objective

We work on our attacking combination play on the flanks with the focus on one-two combinations, 3rd man runs and finishing.

A

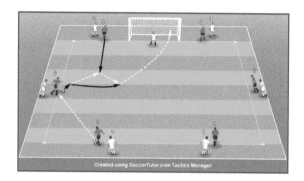

In an area 30 x 30 yards we work with 12 players and a goalkeeper. We have 6 positions with 2 players at each one. We have 2 groups and each group has 3 positions (numbered) with 6 players.

Player 1 passes to player 2 who takes a touch and plays a one-two combination with player 3 who times the run from his position. Player 2 receives, dribbles forward and shoots.

The 2 groups take turns.

B

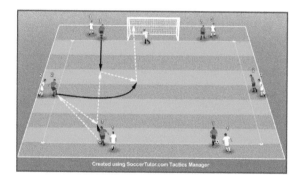

Player 1 plays a one-two combination with player 2 and player 1 passes to player 3 who times the run from his position.

After player 2 plays his pass, he makes a curved run to receive the first time pass from player 3 and shoots.

The 2 groups take turns.

C

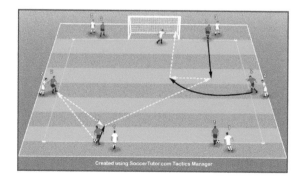

In this variation, player 1 plays a one-two combination with player 2 and then passes diagonally to player 4 who times the run from his position.

While the ball is travelling to player 4, player 3 makes a curved run (3rd man run) to meet the first time pass from player 4 and shoots with 1 touch.

SPAIN Attacking Sessions

PROGRESSION
3. One-Two Combination on the Flanks in a Position Specific Pattern of Play

A

Description

We now use half a pitch and we have 10 players and 12 mannequins in the positions shown in the diagram. The players in the centre are the centre midfielders from the 4-4-2 or the attacking midfielders from the 4-3-3.

The player at the sides can be left/right midfielders from the 4-4-2 or the left/right forwards from the 4-3-3. The other 2 are either strikers from the 4-4-2 or the 1 striker from the 4-3-3 and a wide forward from the 4-3-3.

A:

The practice starts with the player in the centre who passes to the right. The right midfielder takes a directional first touch between the mannequins and plays a one-two combination with one of the attackers who moves across to provide support. The attacker makes a run into the space on the right.

The right midfielder dribbles inside and has 2 options. The first is to shoot and the second is to pass into the space in the penalty area where the other attacker has moved round the mannequin (the attacker shoots with first touch).

SPAIN Attacking Sessions

B

Created using SoccerTutor.com Tactics Manager

B:

In this variation, after the one-two combination, the right midfielder passes the ball into the open space on the right for the run of the attacker out wide.

Now the second attacker makes a run to the near post and the right midfielder moves to the far post.

The first attacker crosses the ball.

Play both drills from both sides.

Coaching Points

The practice should be run as if the mannequins are active defenders so these aspects are key:

1. The correct weight and timing of passes to feet or into space.
2. The directional first touch needs to be out in front of the player, but not too heavy to be dispossessed.
3. Good angles of support play and correct body shape needs to be monitored.
4. The final ball needs to be well timed for the run into the penalty area.
5. The runs into the penalty area need to be coordinated (e.g. one to the near post and one to the far post).

PROGRESSION
4. One-Two Combinations in a Position Specific 11 v 11 Zonal Game

Red Team Low Zone

Created using SoccerTutor.com Tactics Manager

Description

Now we work in the full width of the pitch and 18 yards past the halfway line. The area is divided into 5 zones as shown in the diagram.

The red team have 8 players across the 3 middle zones in a 2-4-2 formation and the whites have 8 players in a 4-2-1-1 formation (from 4-2-3-1). Only 2 white players are allowed in each side zone at a time.

In the low zone for the red team we have the 2 centre backs (playing a high line) and the left and right attacking midfielders for the white team.

The game always starts with the red goalkeeper and the objective is to have good combinations, making sure to use one-two combinations with 3rd man runs to create goal scoring opportunities in the final zone (in behind the defensive line). The player which provides support for the one-two combination must make an opposite movement into space to create an extra solution for the player with the ball.

The white team can only defend in the end zone once the ball is played in there. If they win the ball, they try and score in the opposite goal but they have limited touches or time to do this (6-8 passes or 8-10 seconds).

Rules

1. The 2 red centre backs can support in the possession phase, but are not allowed to enter the central zone.
2. The 2 white attackers only play in transition to attack for the white team (do not defend in possession phase).
3. All red players can enter their low zone in the transition to defence phase.
4. All players have unlimited touches except for the red players in the final zone who have 4-6 seconds to finish.
5. If the white team score the goal counts double.

55

GOAL ANALYSIS

Passing in Behind a Defensive Line Positioned on the Edge of the Box (1)

10-Oct-2009: European Championship 2012 Qualifying

Armenia 1-2 Spain (1st Goal): Torres - Assist: Silva

Spain in a 4-1-4-1 vs Armenia in a 4-4-1-1

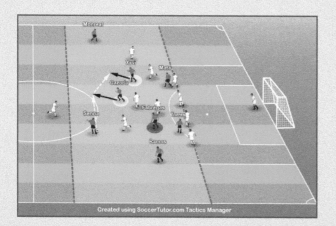

Armenia has 9 players all in the area highlighted and the back 4 are all on the edge of the penalty area with close distances between them. Spain have 8 players in the high zone (2 full backs, 4 midfielders and striker from 4-1-4-1).

Senna has the ball and Cazorla provides support to him by moving back to receive.

Senna passes to Cazorla and Xavi makes the same movement as Cazorla and receives the next pass from him.

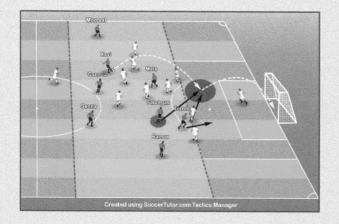

When Xavi receives, Mata also makes a movement back to support him. The right centre back follows him and leaves free space in behind.

Fabregas recognises the situation and wants the ball, so runs into the free space. Xavi plays a quality chipped pass in behind the defensive line into the box.

Fabregas sees the goalkeeper coming off his line and with 1 touch lobs it over him and scores.

GOAL ANALYSIS

Passing in Behind a Defensive Line Positioned on the Edge of the Box (2)

07-Oct-2011: European Championship 2012 Qualifying

Czech Republic 0-2 **Spain (1st Goal):** Mata - Assist: Xavi

Spain in a 4-3-3 vs Czech Republic in a 4-2-3-1

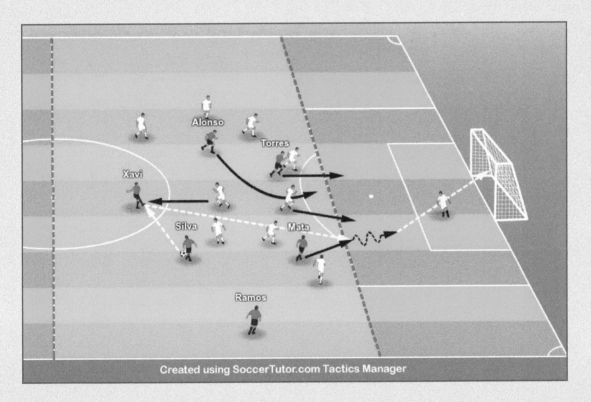

Created using SoccerTutor.com Tactics Manager

Spain have a numerical disadvantage in the high zone, but equal numbers in the area they have the ball.

Silva passes back to Xavi who is in a better position and has a better view to the opposition goal.

While the ball is travelling to Xavi, he sees the free space in behind the defensive line and the poor positioning of the left centre back. He shows very quick decision making and slides a great pass into Mata.

Mata now has the advantage over his opponents and takes a good first touch with his left foot and with the inside of the same foot, scores the goal.

GOAL ANALYSIS

Passing in Behind a Defensive Line Positioned on the Edge of the Box (3)

10-Jun-2012: European Championship 2012 Group Match

Italy 1-1 Spain (1st Goal): Fabregas - Assist: Xavi

Spain in a 4-2-3-1 vs Italy in a 3-5-2

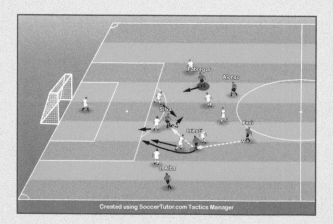

Italy have 3 at the back (3-5-2) and the right centre back closes down Iniesta. Iniesta passes to Silva and asks for the ball again into space (for one-two combination).

The centre back tracks Iniesta's run and Silva takes the ball in the other direction. The other centre back closes him down.

The left back does not move across and there is now a distance between him and the centre back. Fabregas runs forward into the gap.

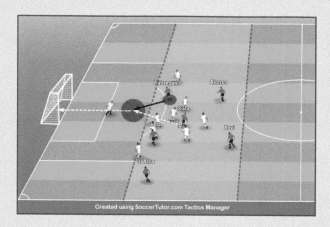

Silva passes through the defence into the penalty area, timed well for the forward run of Fabregas.

Fabregas scores with a 1 touch finish.

58

GOAL ANALYSIS

Passing in Behind a Defensive Line Positioned on the Edge of the Box (4)

01-Jul-2012: European Championship 2012 Final

Spain 4-0 Italy (1st Goal): Fabregas - Assist: Xavi

Spain in a 4-2-3-1 vs Italy in a 4-4-2 (with Diamond)

Italy have an organised defence and Spain constantly play quick, short passes between them.

Arbeloa passes to Silva, Silva to Iniesta and Iniesta back to Silva, Silva to Arbeloa and Arbeloa to Xavi.

After passing to Arbeloa, Silva runs forward to provide support with a different angle (and in behind the opposition's midfield line).

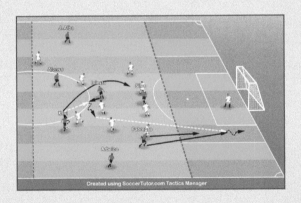

Xavi has an opponent in front so dribbles towards the centre and when he finds space, passes to Iniesta and makes an overlapping run. Iniesta dribbles the ball in the opposite direction. After these passes/movements, the opposition defensive line has a gap between the left back and centre back.

Iniesta and Fabregas recognise the situation and cooperate well. Iniesta plays a quality pass into the box (in behind the back of 4) and Fabregas wins his 1v1 battle to take control of the ball.

Fabregas crosses into the penalty area as Silva runs to the near post and Xavi is running in from behind.

The cross is very quick and Silva gets to the ball first and scores with a header to make it 1-0. This set the way for Spain to win the final.

SPAIN Attacking Sessions

GOAL ANALYSIS

Passing in Behind a Defensive Line Positioned on the Edge of the Box (5)

01-Jul-2012: European Championship 2012 Final

Spain 4-0 Italy (4th Goal): Fabregas - Assist: Xavi

Spain in a 4-2-3-1 vs Italy in a 4-4-2 (with Diamond)

Italy are down to 10 men and have 8 players in the highlighted zone, but play with a very passive defence.

Spain have the full backs, all midfielders and the striker from 4-2-3-1 in the zone highlighted.

Busquets has the ball in the centre and he has space and time to make a forward pass in behind the badly organised (at that moment) Italian defensive line.

Torres runs towards the ball and Mata makes an opposite supporting movement into the penalty area.

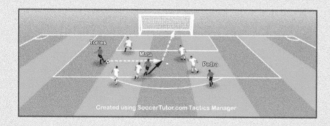

Buffon runs out to pressure Torres, so Torres passes to Mata on his right.

The defenders covering are too slow and Mata scores an easy goal into the empty net.

SESSION FOR THIS TOPIC *(5 Practices)*

Full Pitch Template for 5 Practices

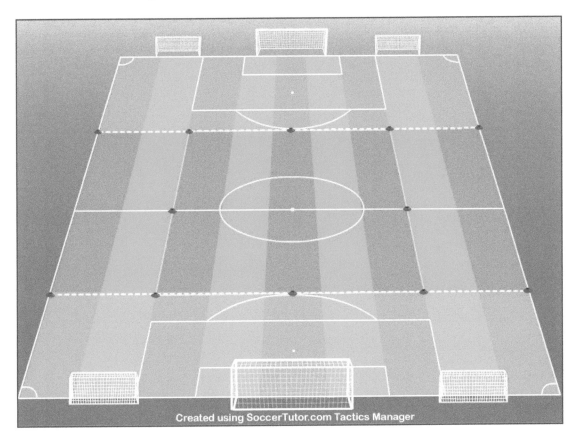

Created using SoccerTutor.com Tactics Manager

Description

Using a full pitch we create 5 zones as shown in the diagram and we have 2 mini goals at each end, positioned at the sides of the full sized goals.

We have 5 different practices numbered from 1-5 and at the beginning we work through them separately.

TOTAL DRILL

Once we have worked through all the exercises, we work on the 'Total Drill'.

The coach calls out the number of a drill (1, 2, 3, 4 or 5) and the teams should be able to recognise it and move very quickly into that particular game situation (from one objective to another).

The practices should be called out by the coach randomly.

1. 6 (+4) v 4 Possession Play in the Centre Transition Game

Objective

We work on maintaining possession in tight areas and quickly switching the play.

Description

We use the area shown and divide it into 2 zones and play a 10v10 game. In one grid we have 10 white players against 4 red. There are 6 white players inside the grid and 4 at the sides (6 (+4) v 4 situation). In the other grid we have the other 6 red players.

The game starts with the white team in possession and the objective for the 6 inside is to complete 4-6 passes, pass to one of the outside support players, then get the ball back to continue their possession. If they achieve all 3 parts, they score 1 point.

If the other team (red) win the ball, they must pass very quickly to the other grid. All the red players and 4 white players move across and the drill continues the same way in the other half.

Different Rules

1. The 6 inside players have unlimited touches and the outside (support) players are limited to 2 touches.
2. The 6 inside players are limited to 3 touches and the outside (support) players are limited to 1 touch.
3. When a team completes 4-6 passes and a player passes to a support player, that support player can pass back to any of the 6 inside players.
4. When a team completes 4-6 passes and a player passes to a support player, that support player can only pass the ball back to the same player who passed to them.

PROGRESSION
2. 10 v 10 Tactical Movements in the Middle Zone Possession Game

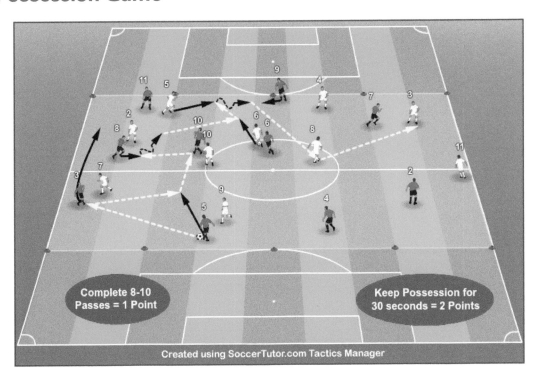

Complete 8-10
Passes = 1 Point

Keep Possession for
30 seconds = 2 Points

Created using SoccerTutor.com Tactics Manager

Objective
We develop possession play in the middle third and can work on specific tactical movements.

Description
We now use the full width of the pitch in the area shown in the diagram. We have 2 teams of 10 players (the red team are in a 4-4-2 formation and the white team are in a 4-3-3 formation). Goals are not used in this drill.

One team starts with the ball and the objective is to try to keep possession under pressure using the full length and width of the zone. The other team defend (press) and if they win the ball, the teams change roles and the game continues in the same way.

If a team completes 8-10 passes they score 1 point and if they keep possession for 30 seconds they score 2 points.

Use this practice to work on tactical movements you want your team to perform when in possession.

Rules
1. All players have unlimited touches.
2. Red team (4-4-2): The centre backs and full backs are limited to 2 touches, the 2 centre midfielders have 3 touches and the wide mifielders and strikers have unlimited touches.
3. White team (4-3-3): The centre backs and full backs are limited to 2 touches, the 2 centre midfielders have 3 touches and the attacking mifielders, wide forwards and the striker have unlimited touches.

SPAIN Attacking Sessions

PROGRESSION
3. 10 v 10 Receiving in Behind the Defence Goal Zone Game

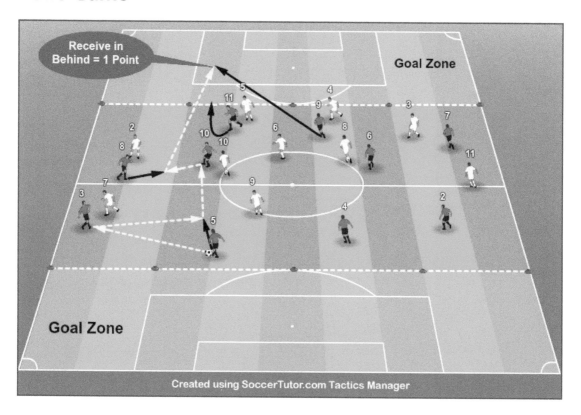

Objective
We work on the same elements as the previous 2 practices, but now we add passing and receiving in behind the defensive line.

Description
In this progression we now use the final thirds on the full pitch. We start in the middle zone and the objective for the team in possession is now to find solutions and use combinations to move the ball in behind the defensive line (into the 'Goal Zone').

The team in possession must play a pass into the 'Goal Zone' and a teammate must receive and have the ball under full control (scores the team 1 point).

Different Rules
1. The defenders are not allowed to enter the 'Goal Zone'.
2. The defenders are allowed in the end zone as soon as the ball is played in there.
3. The coach can either make the team in possession complete 6-8 passes before playing a final ball into the 'Goal Zone' or allow them to pass in there at anytime.

PROGRESSION
4. 10 v 10 Receiving in Behind & Finishing Goal Zone Game

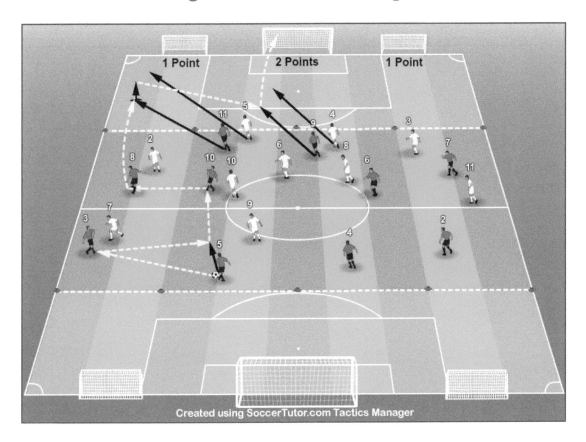

Objective

We work on the same elements as the previous practice, but now the players also practice finishing.

Description

The only difference in this progression is that when the player receives in the 'Goal Zone', he then shoots into 1 of the 3 goals.

To score in the middle goal the player must finish with 1 touch and this scores 2 points. If they score in the small goals at the sides they get 1 point.

The defenders are allowed in the end zone as soon as the ball is played in there.

Coaching Points

1. Players need to use the correct weight/timing of pass, angles and body shape for support play and well timed forward runs to successfully attack in behind the defensive line.
2. Players should display quick and quality finishing with a maximum of 2 touches in the final third.

PROGRESSION
5. 11 v 11 Receiving in Behind & Finishing Goal Zone Game

Created using SoccerTutor.com Tactics Manager

Description

For the final practice in this session we play a normal game. We always start in the middle zone and the objective is to try and score in the full sized goal past the goalkeeper.

Different Rules

1. All players have unlimited touches in the middle zone and 2-3 touches in the final zone.
2. All players have unlimited touches in all zones, but must finish their attack in the final zone within 6-8 seconds.

TOTAL DRILL

After going through all 5 drills we work in the total drill outlined at the beginning of this session.

The coach calls out the number of a practice and the teams should be able to recognise it and move very quickly into that particular game situation (from one objective to another).

The practices should be called out by the coach randomly and not in numerical order.

GOAL ANALYSIS

Attacking on the Flank: Crossing from Deep (1)

15-Oct-2008: World Cup 2010 Qualifying

Belgium 1-2 Spain (2nd Goal): Villa - Assist: Guiza

Spain in a 4-4-2 vs Belgium in a 4-1-4-1 / 4-4-1-1

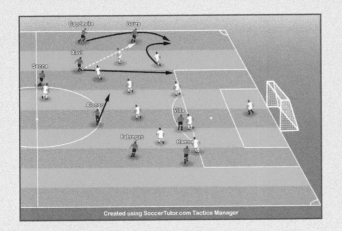

Belgium are in a 4-1-4-1 formation in this phase with good organisation and distances between the lines. Spain would have difficulty to attack through the centre and for this reason attack on the flank.

One attacker (Guiza) uses the width of the pitch and supports the left back (Capdevila).

Xavi passes to Guiza on the left and Capdevila makes an overlapping run. The right back closes him down and Guiza moves the ball onto his right foot.

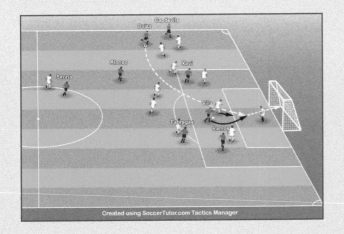

Guiza hits an excellent cross with his right foot in behind the defensive line towards Villa and Ramos who move from the other side into the penalty area.

Villa times his run well and scores with a header.

SPAIN Attacking Sessions

GOAL ANALYSIS

Attacking on the Flank: Crossing from Deep (2)

12-Oct-2010: European Championship 2012 Qualifying

Scotland 2-3 Spain (3rd Goal): Llorente - Assist: Capdevila

Spain in a 4-2-3-1 vs Scotland in a 4-5-1

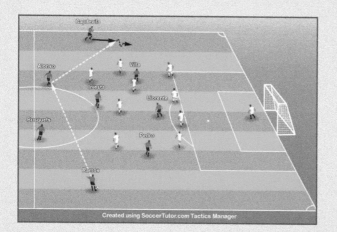

We have the same situation again here. Scotland have 9 players in the low zone with good organisation and distances between the lines. They have closed the space in the centre of the pitch.

Spain attack on the flank. The full backs are out wide and the 2-3-1 part of the formation play inside.

The ball goes from the right flank to the left side to change the direction of the attack. Ramos passes to Alonso and he pass to the left back (Capdevila).

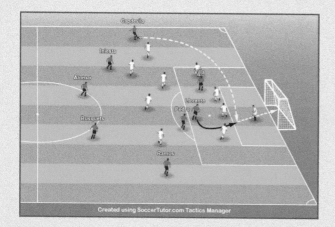

Capdevila hits a good cross in behind the defensive line and Llorente makes a well timed run into the penalty area and scores with a volley.

GOAL ANALYSIS

Attacking on the Flank: Crossing from Deep (3)

18-Jun-2008: European Championship 2008 Qualifying

Spain 2-1 Greece (2nd Goal): Guiza - Assist: Sergio

Spain in a 4-2-3-1 vs Greece in a 5-4-1 / 3-6-1 (3-4-2-1 in attacking phase)

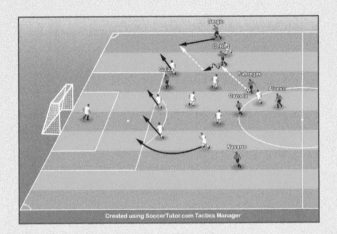

Greece have many players in the centre of the pitch and Spain play the ball from the middle to the right flank.

Fabregas (attacking midfielder) passes to the centre midfielder who dribbles forward and passes to Sergio high up on the right flank.

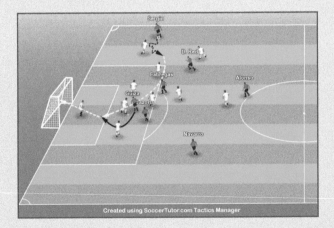

Sergio receives, moves the ball to his left foot and crosses the ball into the penalty area.

Guiza shows good movement, wins the battle with his opponent and scores with a header.

GOAL ANALYSIS

Attacking on the Flank: Crossing from Deep (4)

08-Oct-2010: European Championship 2012 Qualifying

Spain 3-1 Lithuania (3rd Goal): Silva - Assist: Ramos

Spain in a 4-1-4-1 vs Lithuania in a 4-4-2

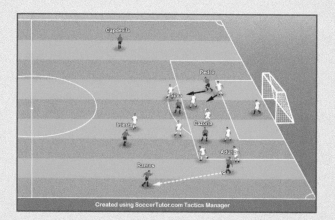

Lithuania have 8 players in and around the penalty area.

Aduriz is under pressure from the left back and passes the ball back to Ramos

Ramos has free space in front of him and 4 teammates.

While the ball is travelling to Ramos, Pedro runs back to avoid being offside.

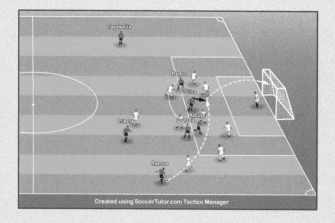

Ramos makes a quick technical cross and Silva times his run well into the space.

Silva heads the ball brilliantly into the top right hand corner of the goal.

SESSION FOR THIS TOPIC *(4 Practices)*

1. Full Back's Support Play in a 9 v 9 (+2) End to End Possession Game

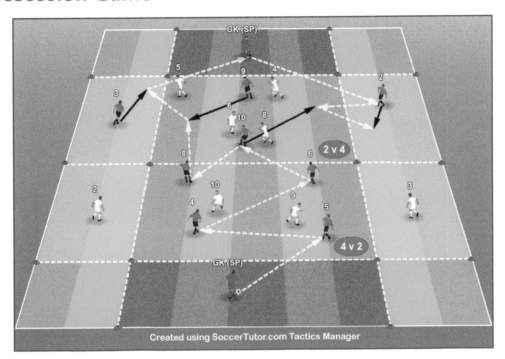

Created using SoccerTutor.com Tactics Manager

Objective
We work on keeping possession in this position specific practice with the focus on using the full backs out wide.

Description
In an area 45 x 45 yards we divide the pitch into 6 zones in the middle and 2 end zones. In the middle we have 4 side zones which are 14 x 8 yards each and 2 central zones which are 14 x 28 yards each. We also have the 2 end zones which are 8 x 28 yards. We have an 8v8 situation with 2 support goalkeepers at the ends.

In the low central zone for each team we have a 4v2 situation, (2 centre backs & 2 centre midfielders from the 4-4-2) and in the high central zone there is a 2v4 situation (2 strikers from 4-4-2). In the side high zones we have 1 side player for each team (full backs).

Both teams aim to keep possession and transfer the ball from one goalkeeper to another. If this happens they score 1 point. The players must use the side players in the central high zone, otherwise they have a numerical disadvantage.

Rules
1. The centre backs, centre midfielders and full backs are limited to 2-3 touches and the strikers have unlimited touches.
2. The players are not allowed to leave their respective zones.

PROGRESSION

2. Full Back's Support Play in a 10 v 10 (+2) End to End Possession Game on a Full Pitch

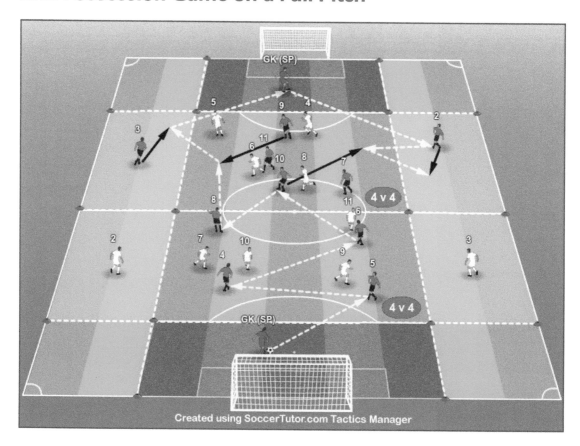

Created using SoccerTutor.com Tactics Manager

Description

We now play the same game using a full pitch. We create the 6 zones again as shown in the diagram.

We also add the wide midfielders (right and left) for both teams and they play within the central high zone to create 4v4 situations in these areas.

The rules and objectives remain the same. The goals are not in use as the goalkeepers are still acting as support players.

Coaching Points

1. This practice should include quick and quality short passes to feet and into space.
2. The correct body shape should be monitored (opening up) and receiving/passing with the back foot (foot furthest away from the ball).
3. Good awareness and quick decision making is required in this game (pressure of time and space).

PROGRESSION
3. Crossing from Deep in a Position Specific Zonal Game

Created using SoccerTutor.com Tactics Manager

Description

For this progression we add 2 full sized goals.

The objective is to play using the sides (full backs) and cross the ball into the penalty area. All players from the high central zone can then move into the penalty area to score from the cross.

PROGRESSION

4. Crossing from Deep in a Position Specific Zonal Game (2)

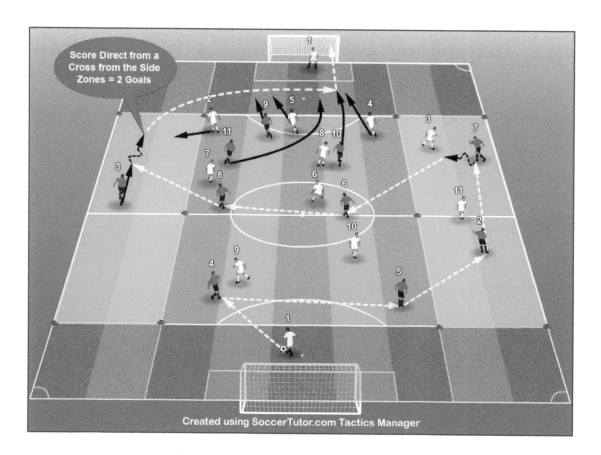

Description

In this final practice of the session we play a normal 11v11 game. The red team are in a 4-4-2 and the white team are in a 4-3-3.

If a team scores a goal they get 1 point and if they score directly from a cross (from the sides zones) the goal counts double.

GOAL ANALYSIS

Attacking on the Flank: Crossing from the Byline (1)

08-Oct-2010: European Championship 2012 Qualifying

Spain 3-1 Lithuania (1st Goal): Guiza - Assist: Sergio

Spain in a 4-1-4-1 vs Lithuania in a 4-4-2

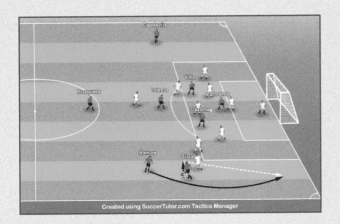

In this situation Spain force the opposition back and Lithuania have 9 players inside or near to the penalty area.

Spain attack on the flank again. Silva has the ball and Ramos makes an overlapping run to create a numerical advantage (2v1) on the right side.

Silva dribbles inside to create space for Ramos (attracting the defender) and at the correct time he passes into the space to Ramos.

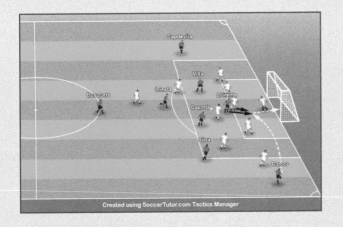

Ramos receives the pass and Spain have 6 players in and around the penalty area.

Ramos crosses to the near post, Llorente wins the 1v1 battle with the defender and scores the goal.

SPAIN Attacking Sessions

GOAL ANALYSIS

Attacking on the Flank: Crossing from the Byline (2)

08-Oct-2010: European Championship 2012 Qualifying

Spain 3-1 Lithuania (2nd Goal): Llorente - Assist: Cazorla

Spain in a 4-1-4-1 vs Lithuania in a 4-4-2

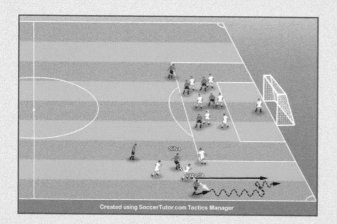

We have the same situation as the previous one.

Silva passes to Cazorla on the right flank and he dribbles the ball forward in a 1v1 situation.

Cazorla uses feints and changes direction to beat the opponent.

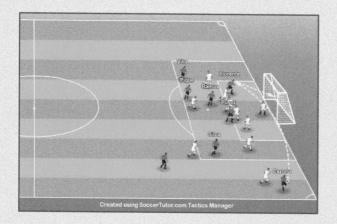

Spain have 6 players in the penalty area.

Cazorla crosses the ball to the far post into a space where Llorente wins the aerial battle and scores again.

GOAL ANALYSIS

Attacking on the Flank: Crossing from the Byline (3)

11-Oct-2011: European Championship 2012 Qualifying

Spain 3-1 Scotland (1st Goal): Silva - Assist: J. Alba

Spain in a 4-3-3 vs Scotland in a 4-4-2

Scotland are very compact in 2 lines of defence within the width of the penalty area. Spain have limited space in the centre to pass forwards.

Xavi plays a one-two combination with Silva and he recognises the situation in the centre, so plays the ball to Villa on the left flank (using the full width).

After his pass back to Xavi, Silva runs forward into a new attacking position.

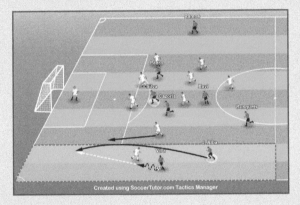

Villa dribbles forward with an opponent (right back) in front of him.

J. Alba makes a supporting run (as shown) to create a 2v1 numerical advantage against the right back.

Villa passes the ball down the line into the space. The right centre back stays in the centre and does not support the right back, so the right midfielder tracks J. Alba's run in behind.

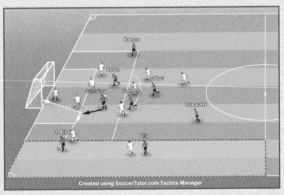

J. Alba gets to the ball first and with his first touch he plays a short cross to Silva who has timed his run into the penalty area.

Silva hits a great first time shot to score at the near post.

SPAIN Attacking Sessions

SESSION FOR THIS TOPIC *(3 Practices)*

1. Continuous Crossing & Finishing Practice

Created using SoccerTutor.com Tactics Manager

Objective

To develop crossing, heading, defending crosses, attacking crosses and runs/movement within the penalty area.

Description

We use an area double the size of the penalty area and have 2 full sized goals. We work with 2 teams of 5, 2 goalkeepers and 4 neutral players at the sides of the pitch. The neutrals have a ball each (or multiple balls).

The 2 yellow neutrals cross for goal 1 and the other two (blue) cross for goal 2. The red team score in goal 1 and defend goal 2. The white team score in goal 2 and defend goal 1.

The practice starts with one team in the attacking phase. The neutral from the right crosses the ball into the penalty area for the reds to score in goal 1. There is a 5v5 battle in front of the goal. When the attack is finished or the ball goes out of play, the next neutral from the left side crosses a new ball into the same area.

When the attack is finished or the ball goes out of play, all players move towards goal 2. The teams change roles and we have a 5v5 situation again with the other 2 neutral players taking turns to cross the ball.

PROGRESSION

2. Crossing & Finishing with Quick Transitional Wide Counter Attacks

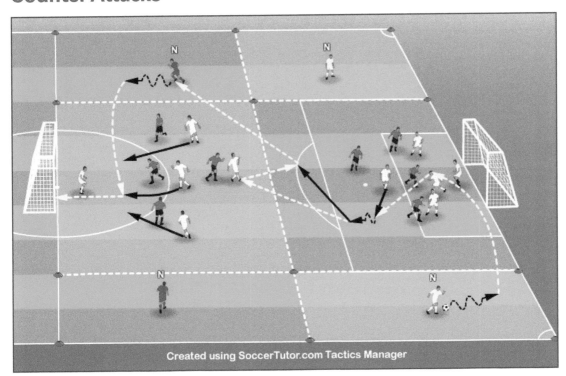

Created using SoccerTutor.com Tactics Manager

Objective

We have the same elements as the previous practice, but now also work on quick transitions to attack out wide.

Description

In this progression we expand to use half of a full pitch and mark out the zones as shown in the diagram. We now have a 4v4 situation in each central zone, but we still have the same 4 neutral players in the side zones. All players must stay within their zone and can only shoot in their goal.

The practice starts with one team in possession and the objective is to quickly pass the ball to a teammate in the other zone and attack by using the 2 neutrals in the side zones. The neutrals cross the ball in and there is a 4v4 situation with the attackers trying to score (1 point).

The defenders try to clear the ball so the team can make a fast transition from defence to attack with the same objective (they pass to the other zone, then to a neutral player out wide who crosses the ball).

Coaching Points

1. Players should coordinate their runs - e.g. One to the near post, one far post and 1 running in from behind.

2. Monitor the movements inside the penalty area and encourage players to finish with 1 touch.

3. The accuracy, weight and timing of the crosses are key for this practice to be successful.

SPAIN Attacking Sessions

PROGRESSION
3. 2 v 1 Flank Play in a Dynamic Zonal Game

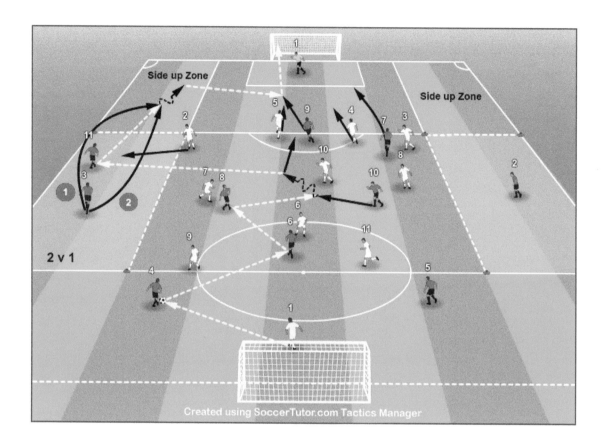

Description

Working on a full pitch, we place a full sized goal 18 yards past the halfway line. The middle zone between the penalty area and the halfway line is divided into 3 zones as shown in the diagram.

We play an 11v11 game with the red team in a 4-3-3 formation (with V) and the white team in a 4-4-2 (with bowl). Only the full backs on both teams and the red wide forwards are allowed in the side zones.

The objective for the red team is to use the side zones (full width of the pitch) to create a numerical advantage (2v1) on the flanks and cross from near the byline to score.

If the red team score a goal by attacking through the centre they get 1 point and if they score a goal after a cross/pass from the side zone, they get 2 points.

If the white team win the ball, they must finish their counter attack within 10 seconds.

When an attack is finished or the ball goes out of play, it always restarts with the red goalkeeper. After a set amount of time, change the roles of the teams.

GOAL ANALYSIS

Creating Space to Shoot from Outside the Box (1)

18-Jun-2008: European Championship 2008 Qualifying

Spain 2-1 Greece (2nd Goal): D.Red - Assist: Guiza

Spain in a 4-2-3-1 vs Greece in a 5-4-1 / 3-6-1 (3-4-2-1 in attacking phase)

Greece have 9 players (in a 3-6 formation) in front of the ball in 2 zones.

Fabregas plays a chipped pass to Guiza and takes the first zone of 6 players out of the game.

While the ball is travelling to Guiza, D. Red and Cazorla move forward to support him and receive a pass back.

This creates a 3v3 situation.

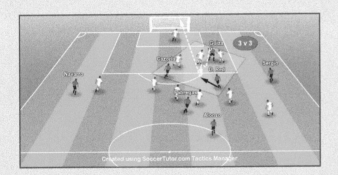

Guiza wins the aerial battle against the Greek defender and heads the ball back on to the edge of the penalty area where Cazorla and D.Red are arriving.

D. Red hits a first time volley and scores a brilliant goal.

SPAIN Attacking Sessions

SESSION FOR THIS TOPIC *(4 Practices)*

1. Creating Space to Shoot Using a Target Man in an Unopposed Pattern of Play

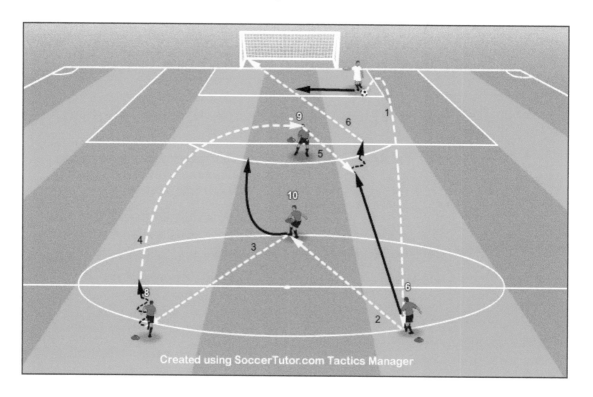

Created using SoccerTutor.com Tactics Manager

Objective

To develop attacking combination play, the striker's hold up play (target man) and shooting from distance.

Description

We work with 4 players in half a full pitch. We have 2 cones in the centre midfield position, one for the attacking midfielder and one in a striker's position. The 2 centre midfielders, 1 attacking midfielder and 1 striker are from the 4-2-3-1 formation.

The goalkeeper starts and makes a long pass to one of the centre midfielders. The centre midfielder controls the ball and passes to the attacking midfielder who passes to the other centre midfielder.

The second centre midfielder then plays a long aerial pass to the striker. While the ball is travelling to the striker, the attacking midfielder and the first centre midfielder run forward to support the striker to the left and right of him.

The striker heads the ball down to one of these players who control the ball and shoot at goal.

PROGRESSION

2. Creating Space to Shoot Using a Target Man in an Opposed Pattern of Play

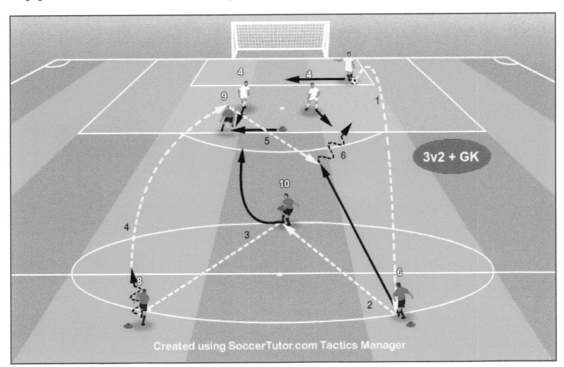

Objective

To develop attacking combination play, the striker's hold up play (target man) and shooting from distance under pressure from 2 defenders.

Description

For this progression we add 2 defenders (centre backs) behind the striker who defend the goal.

The first defender just challenges the striker in the aerial battle (1v1) and the second presses the midfielder who runs up to shoot at goal. The second defender can only press within the penalty area and is not allowed to leave it.

Coaching Points

1. The accuracy and height of the chipped pass is key, to allow the striker to win the aerial battle and head the ball down for a teammate.
2. The 2 support players need to move forward quickly, but also need to arrive into the space at the correct time and should adjust their strides (length of steps) accordingly.
3. The players should look to shoot as quickly as possible before the defender is able to close the angle to goal.

PROGRESSION
3. Creating Space to Shoot Using a Target Man in a 7 v 6 Zonal Game

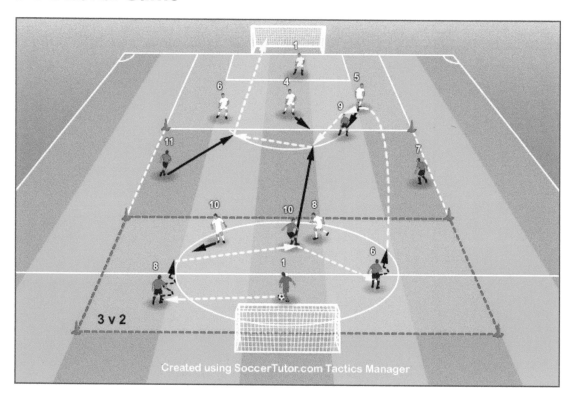

Created using SoccerTutor.com Tactics Manager

Objective

We work on attacking combination play, the striker's hold up play (target man) and shooting from distance under pressure within a small sided game.

Description

We now place another full sized goal 10-12 yards from the halfway line and we create 3 zones as shown in the diagram.

In the first zone we have a 3v2 situation with 2 centre midfielders and 1 attacking midfielder from the 4-2-3-1 against 2 opposition centre midfielders. In the second zone we have the 2 attacking midfielders and the striker. In the final zone (penalty area) we have 3 opposition centre backs (from the 3-5-2 or 5-4-1).

The game starts with the red goalkeeper and we have a 3v2 situation. They must play a chipped pass to the striker on the edge of the area. 1 or 2 players must then quickly move to support the striker. If the 2 white players win the ball, they try to score (in a 2v3 situation) and if they do the goal counts double.

One of the attacking midfielders in the middle zone supports the striker and the other does the same if the second centre midfielder does not run forward to support.

The 3 centre backs play active defence for the aerial challenge and try to stop/block the shot, but they are not allowed to leave the penalty area.

PROGRESSION
4. Creating Space to Shoot Using a Target Man in a 9 v 10 Zonal Game

Description

In this progression we extend the area to the full width of the pitch as shown in the diagram.

We have a normal game with the red team in a 2-2-3-1 formation (from the 4-2-3-1 without the 2 centre backs) and the white team are in a 5-4 formation (from 5-4-1).

The game always starts with the red goalkeeper and we play an 8v10 game.

The basic objective is to pass the ball from the low zone with a chipped pass to the striker (through or over the opposition midfield line) and a minimum of 2 players should make runs forward to support.

The red team must find solutions to finish their attack. 3 routes to goal are shown in the diagram.

GOAL ANALYSIS

Creating Space to Shoot from Outside the Box (2)

03-Sep-2010: European Championship 2012 Qualifying

Liechtenstein 0-4 **Spain (2nd Goal):** Villa - Assist: Alonso

Spain in a 4-4-2 vs Liechtenstein in a 4-2-3-1

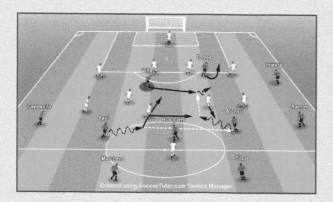

Capdevila and Ramos (full backs) provide the width, the 3 midfielders are inside and Iniesta is on the right flank to create a numerical superiority on this side of the pitch.

Xavi dribbles inside to find forward passing options, but is under pressure and passes to Alonso. Alonso does the same and passes to Villa who moves across to receive. This combination takes 6 Liechtenstein players out of the game.

Torres runs towards the right, creating space for Villa and provides an extra passing option.

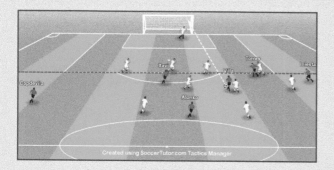

Villa takes a touch out of his feet and scores with a 25 yard strike.

GOAL ANALYSIS

Creating Space to Shoot from Outside the Box (3)

19-Sep-2008: World Cup 2010 Qualifying

Spain 4-0 Armenia (4th Goal): Senna - Assist: Iniesta

Spain in a 4-4-2 vs Armenia in a 4-4-2

We have the same situation as the previous one. Capdevila and Ramos provide the width and the midfielders/attackers play inside to give the ball carrier many angles of support (in front, behind and to the side).

Alonso has the ball and Iniesta moves to support him. Iniesta receives the pass, turns and when the centre midfielder closes him down, he passes to Senna on the right.

Senna runs into the space, controls the ball and dribbles forwards.

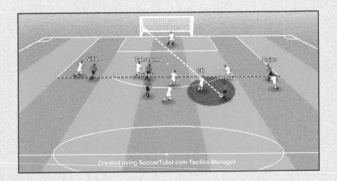

The Armenian centre back (CB) is slow to close down Senna so he has the time and space to shoot from 25 yards and scores to make it 4-0.

SPAIN Attacking Sessions

GOAL ANALYSIS

Creating Space to Shoot from Outside the Box (4)

25-Mar-2011: European Championship 2012 Qualifying.

Spain 2-1 Czech Republic (1st Goal): Villa - Assist: Iniesta

Spain in a 4-3-3 vs Czech Republic in a 4-2-3-1

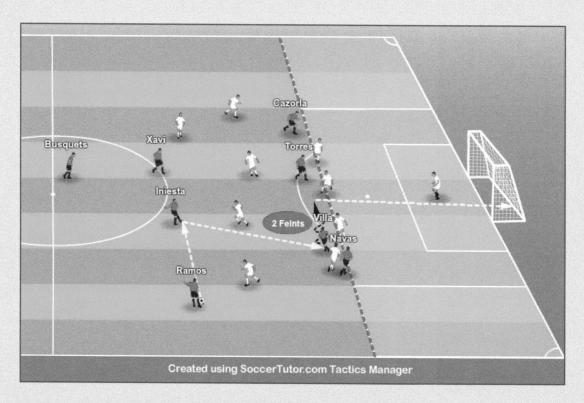

The opponents are defending close to the penalty area with 2 lines (defence and midfield) very close to each other. There is a 4v4 situation on the edge of the box.

Ramos passes to Iniesta and he passes quickly to Villa who receives and dribbles parallel to the goal, moving the ball onto his left foot.

Villa is under pressure of time and space and uses 2 feints to create half a yard of space. He produces an excellent low shot into the bottom corner and scores.

SESSION FOR THIS TOPIC *(3 Practices)*

1. Attacking through the Centre in a 4 Zone Shooting Game

Created using SoccerTutor.com Tactics Manager

Objective

To develop quick forward passing through the midfield line and shooting.

Description

In an area 40 x 30 yards, we divide the pitch into 4 zones (10 x 30 yards each). We have 2 full sized goals with goalkeepers and we work with 12 outfield players (6v6). There are 3 players in each zone as shown and they are not allowed to leave their respective zone at any point.

The objective is to pass the ball forward through the opponent's first line of 3 and work a way to shoot at goal under pressure from the final 3 opponents who try to prevent or block the shot (from within their zone).

Rule

All players have unlimited (or 2-3) touches.

PROGRESSION

2. Attacking through the Centre in a 4 Zone Shooting Game (2)

1 Player can leave this zone

Created using SoccerTutor.com Tactics Manager

Description

In this progression we just make 1 small change. Now when a team passes the ball from the low to the high zone, one of the 3 white defenders whose zone they have passed through can leave their zone to apply pressure from behind (as shown in the diagram).

This rule forces the red players to shoot (finish their attack) quickly as it is now a 3 v 3 (+1) situation and they have less time and space.

Coaching Points

1. The players need to take a good directional first touch (get the ball out of their feet) to shoot quickly before the player behind closes them down or the defenders in front block the angle to goal.

2. Players should use 1 touch combinations when possible to move the opposition players around so that gaps are created and it is easier to pass the ball through their line.

PROGRESSION

3. Attacking through the Centre and Shooting from Distance in a 6 v 6 Dynamic Small Sided Game

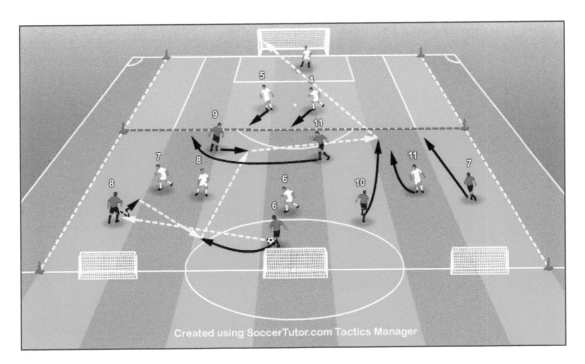

Created using SoccerTutor.com Tactics Manager

Objective

To develop quick forward passing through the midfield line and shooting from distance under pressure in a small sided game.

Description

For the final drill in this session we work in the area shown and place 3 mini goals at one end and a full sized goal at the other. It is a 6v6 game with a goalkeeper in the full sized goal.

The red team are in a 4-2 formation (from 4-4-2) with 4 midfielders and 2 strikers, but you can also use a 3-3 (from 4-3-3). The white team are in a 2-2-2 formation with 2 centre backs, 2 centre midfielders and 2 attacking midfielders from the 4-2-3-1. The 2 white centre backs only move within the height of the penalty area.

The red team try to find a solution to finish their attack from outside the box. In the main area there is a 6v4 numerical advantage and they must use good movement and provide good support angles to the player with the ball. If they can score from outside of the penalty area they get 2 points.

The white team try to win the ball and then score in the 3 mini goals on the halfway line (1 point). The centre backs can play in the counter attack but must stay in their zone. When/if the reds lose the ball, they must move quickly from attack to defence (negative transition).

SPAIN Attacking Sessions

GOAL ANALYSIS

Individual Play: Dribbling & Creativity

21-Jun-2010: World Cup 2010 Qualifying

Spain 2-0 Honduras (1st Goal): Villa

Spain in a 4-3-3 vs Honduras in a 4-2-3-1

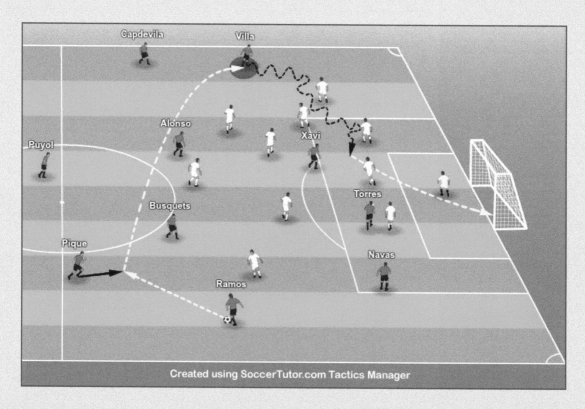

Created using SoccerTutor.com Tactics Manager

Spain have the ball in the opposition half and Honduras defend in the low zone. The ball is moved from Ramos to Pique who plays a long ball to switch the point of attack from the right to the left side.

Villa receives and shows great technique and creativity in his individual attack. With good quality dribbling and feints, he passes the ball in between the first 2 opponents and when he gets into the penalty area, he is faced with a final 1v1 with the right centre back.

Taking advantage of his speed, Villa feints and moves the ball onto his right foot and finishes into the far corner of the net.

SESSION FOR THIS TOPIC *(3 Practices)*

1. Dribbling Inside from the Flank and Shooting Unopposed

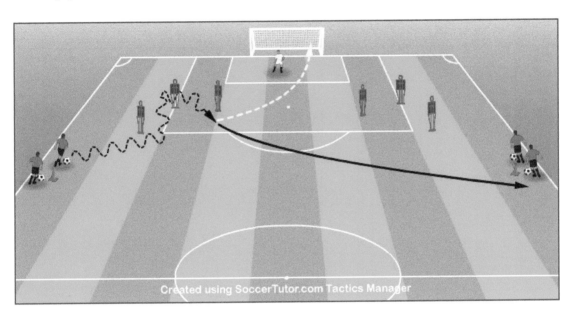

Created using SoccerTutor.com Tactics Manager

Objective
To develop dribbling inside from the flank to beat opponents and create space to shoot in the penalty area.

Description
Here we work with 2 groups (left and right of the penalty area) and we put 3 mannequins in each corner of the penalty area as shown in the diagram.

Each player dribbles in and out of the 3 mannequins as shown using good quality control of the ball and when they go past the last mannequin, they shoot at goal.

Start off slowly and progress the players to dribbling with high speed.

Coaching Points
1. There needs to be high quality and speed when dribbling the ball with soft touches.
2. Players should look to see the goalkeeper's position to see which corner is best to shoot in and try to score in there.

PROGRESSION

2. Switching Play & Finishing in a Continuous 1 v 1 Duel Practice

PART 1

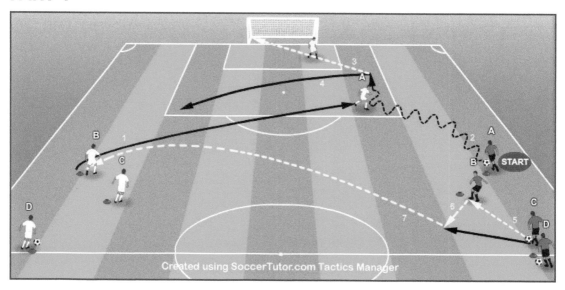

PART 2

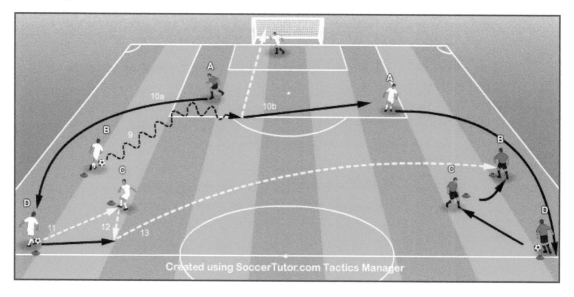

SPAIN Attacking Sessions

Objective

To develop dribbling, 1v1 play, combination play and switching play.

Description

We work with an equal number of players on each side (a total of 8 minimum).

Part 1 - As shown in the diagram, we start on the right and the white player A from the left group moves over to be a defender in the corner of the penalty area. The first attacker (red A) from the right group goes into a 1v1 with him.

When the first player finishes his attack, the red players C & B from the right side play a one-two combination and then C plays a long ball to switch the play.

Part 2 - The second player from the left side (B) receives and dribbles up to the penalty area. The attacker (red A) who had the shot moves across to be the defender for the new 1v1 (quick transition from attack to defence).

When white player B finishes his attack, white player D and C play a one-two combination and then D plays a long ball to switch the play.

Red player B then receives on the right side and goes into a 1v1 against white player B who moves across to defend after shooting.

The players always move across to defend after shooting. After defending, they then move into the player D position on the opposite side (as shown by both Player A's curved runs in the part 2 diagram).

PROGRESSION

3. Double 1 v 1 Play on the Flank & Finishing in a Dynamic Side Zone Practice

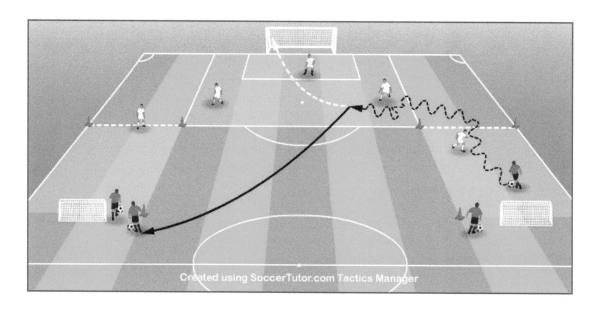

Created using SoccerTutor.com Tactics Manager

Objective

To develop dribbling, 1 v 1 play and shooting within the penalty area.

Description

We now create 2 zones at the sides as shown in the diagram. We also add 1 mini goal on each side.

The practice starts with the attacker who has the ball (in the diagram) and he is in a 1v1 situation with the objective to beat the first defender. If the defender wins the ball, they try to score in the mini goal and the attacker moves quickly into transition from attack to defence.

If the attacker beats the defender and passes through the line (white dashes), they go into another 1v1 with the next defender in the penalty area and shoot at goal.

The attackers swap sides after their shot at goal.

Coaching Points

1. Encourage the players to be creative and try using different feints/moves to beat in this practice.
2. In the 1v1 duels, the ball carrier should make sure to have the correct body shape and use their body as a barrier between their opponent and the ball.
3. Players should look to shoot quickly as soon as they enter the penalty area.

96

CHAPTER 2

Attacking Against Teams which Defend in the Middle Zone

Attacking Against Teams which Defend in the Middle Zone

Spain scored 10 goals in this game situation against teams who defended in the middle zone and we can put them into 3 categories:

1. Spain scored with good combination play

In this situation we have a high quality passing game between 2-3 (or more) players with continuous passing and movement. In most cases there were short passes to feet and one-two combinations, waiting until the right moment to play a final pass into the space in behind the defensive line.

2. Attacking through the lines

Spain built up play from the back and switch the ball (from left to right and via versa) with the objective to change the balance of the opposition's organisation of their midfield and defensive lines. At the right time one player moved and asked for the ball in behind the midfield to receive a pass from a teammate. This would take up to 6 opposition players out of the game and that player would only have 4 defenders in front of him.

3. Keeping possession in the middle zone before playing a long ball in behind the defensive line

One player would make the run (normally a wide midfielder or attacking midfielder) in between a full back and centre back and receive the long pass in the penalty area. The nearest player (normally the striker) would make a run to the far past for the short cross and the other teammates would run forward into the penalty area to support.

GOAL ANALYSIS

Attacking Combination Play: Switching Positions to Create Space

10-Jun-2008: European Championship 2008 Qualifying

Spain 4-1 Russia (3rd Goal): Villa - Assist: Fabregas

Spain in a 4-1-3-2 vs Russia in a 3-4-1-2 (from 70 minutes)

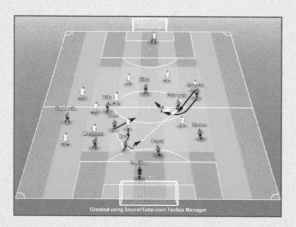

Spain have the ball with Senna who passes back to Xavi. In the middle zone and in the centre of the pitch there are a lot of players from both teams. Xavi passes forward to Fabregas.

While the ball is travelling, Cazorla makes an opposite movement from outside to inside and runs in front of Fabregas. Fabregas passes to him and runs in the opposite direction into the free space created by Cazorla. This movement from Cazorla creates defensive imbalance and makes it very difficult for the defenders. Cazorla dribbles forward with the ball.

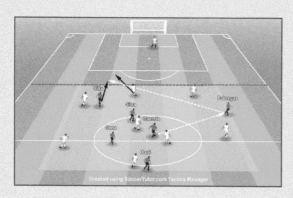

Cazorla passes to Fabregas in the space on the right.

Fabregas has the time and space to pass in between the 2 defenders and in behind them, into an area Villa is running into.

Villa receives the pass in behind and dribbles into the penalty area using feints and changes of direction (individual attack).

Villa finishes well into the near post and scores the goal.

SESSION FOR THIS TOPIC *(5 Practices)*

1. Switching Positions to Create Space in a Combination Pattern of Play

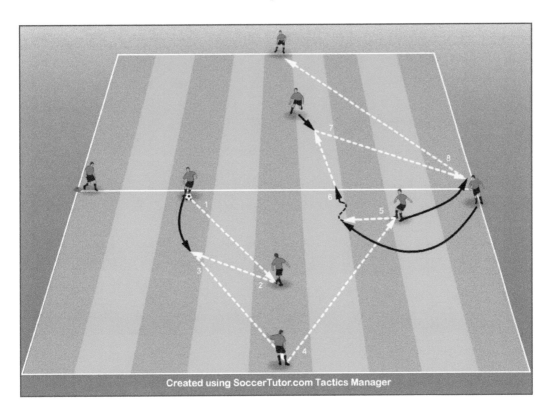

Created using SoccerTutor.com Tactics Manager

Objective

To develop the correct weight/timing of passing/movement necessary for this specific attacking combination.

Description

In an area 28 x 14 yards we divide the pitch into 2 grids. We work with 8 players in a pattern of play. There are always 4 players at the sides of the grid (in the positions shown in the diagram) and 4 players inside.

This formation must be kept continuously for the duration of the practice regardless of the consecutive switches of position. The positioning of the players creates 2 diamonds.

The objective is to repeat the same combination as shown in the analysis between Cazorla and Fabregas. All the passes and movements are displayed in the diagram in number order. Players are limited to 2 touches.

The players pass the ball with good rhythm and focus on the cooperation of the 2 players at the sides. While the 4th pass is travelling, the player at the side makes a curved run in front of the next player and receives the next pass from them. That player then switches and takes up the position on the side (in and out combination).

©SoccerTutor.com

SPAIN Attacking Sessions

PROGRESSION

2. Switching Positions to Create Space in a 6 v 6 (+4) End to End Possession Game

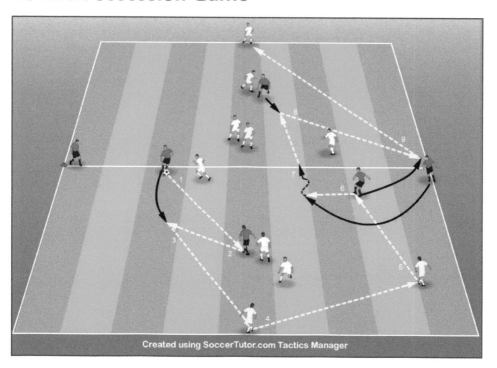

Created using SoccerTutor.com Tactics Manager

Objective

We work on the same combination as the previous drill, but now with the pressure of keeping possession against 6 defending players.

Description

We progress the pattern of play and now have 2 teams of 6 players and 4 neutral players. 1 neutral is at each end and the other 2 play inside. The team which has possession (red team in diagram) have 4 players inside and 2 players at the sides. The other team (whites) have all players 6 inside the grid.

The objective is to keep possession and complete 6-8 passes to score 1 point. If they are able to achieve this with the same combination shown in the previous pattern of play they score 2 points. The combination can also be done between a side player and a neutral player, but in this case another inside player must recognise the situation and run quickly to replace the player in the side position.

If the white team win the ball, the teams change roles and 2 white players move immediately to the sides and 4 stay inside (and all reds move inside).

Different Rules

1. The team in possession have unlimited touches and the neutrals are limited to 2 touches.
2. The team in possession are limited to 3 touches and the neutrals have 2 touches.
3. The team in possession are limited to 2 touches and the neutrals have 1 touch.

PROGRESSION
3. Switching Positions to Create Space in a 7 v 7 (+4) Possession and Finishing Game with Central Zone

Created using SoccerTutor.com Tactics Manager

Objective
We work on the same attacking combination within a small sided game.

Description
Using a full pitch now, we are working with the same 16 players and create a middle zone in the area shown in the diagram. The objective is to play the same combination as shown in the rest of the session and complete 6-8 passes.

The difference here is that when they have completed 6-8 passes, they now leave the zone to attack and try to score in the goal past the goalkeeper.

Different Rules
1. We use the same rules as the previous practice.
2. The defending team's players are not allowed to leave the zone, but the attacker has limited touches or time to finish (e.g. 2-3 touches or 4-6 seconds).
3. 2 attackers and 1 defender can leave the zone. The attackers have 2 touches outside the zone, but must finish with 1 touch.
4. All players are allowed to leave the zone once the ball is played out.

SPAIN Attacking Sessions

PROGRESSION

4. Switching Positions to Create Space in a 9 v 9 Possession and Finishing Game with Central Zone

Created using SoccerTutor.com Tactics Manager

Description

Using a full pitch again, we now mark out a bigger zone 55 x 50 yards as shown in the diagram. We no longer have any neutral players and have an 8v8 situation within the zone with 2 white centre backs who must stay on the line. Neither teams have full backs and they both use a 2-3-3 formation.

The objective is to play the same combination as shown in the rest of the session and attempt to complete 6-8 passes. When they have completed 6-8 passes, they leave the zone to attack and try to score in the goal.

Different Rules

1. The 2 centre backs are not allowed to follow the ball out of the zone and the attackers are limited to 2-3 touches before shooting.

2. The 2 centre backs are allowed to defend outside of the zone, but only once the ball is played out.

Coaching Points

1. Encourage players to use the specific combination (switching positions - inside/outside).

2. Players should use 1 touch whenever possible to maximise the speed of play.

PROGRESSION

5. Switching Positions Attacking Combination Play in an 11 v 10 Position Specific Game with Central Zone

Created using SoccerTutor.com Tactics Manager

Objective

We work on the same attacking combination in a position specific game on a full pitch.

Description

The final game in this session is 11v10. We add 2 red full backs and a third centre back for the white team. The red team are in a 4-1-3-2 formation and the white team are in a 3-4-2.

The game starts with the red team and their objective is to play the same combination as shown in the rest of the session and attempt to complete 6-8 passes. When they have completed 6-8 passes, they leave the zone to attack and try to score in the goal. The whites try to win the ball and attack. The game always restarts with reds.

Different Rules

1. The 3 white centre backs are not allowed to follow the ball out of the zone and the attackers are limited to 2-3 touches before shooting.
2. The 3 white centre backs are allowed to defend outside of the zone, but only once the ball is played out.

Coaching Points

1. We again focus on opposite movements, with 1 player moving inside and the other outside.
2. Players should vary their passes - passes to feet and passes into space.
3. The white team should demonstrate good and collective defensive organisation in the centre of the pitch.

GOAL ANALYSIS

Attacking Combination Play: Maintaining Possession Before Quickly Switching Play to the Opposition's Weak Side (1)

14-Oct-2009: World Cup 2010 Qualifying

Bosnia Hz 2-5 Spain (2nd Goal): Silva - Assist: Negredo

Spain in a 4-1-4-1 vs Bosnia Hz in a 4-1-3-2

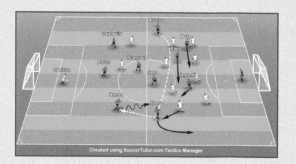

Alonso takes a free kick and plays a long ball to switch the attack from left to right. The opposition are in a 4-4 formation, all behind the ball.

While the ball is travelling to Iraola, the opposition's left midfielder closes him down. Iraola plays a first time pass back to Ramos who has free space and dribbles the ball forward. The aim was to disrupt the organisation and create a numerical superiority.

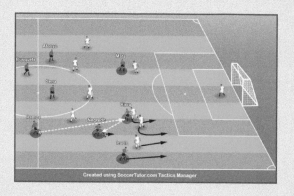

Iraola goes wide, Negredo wants the ball and Riera and Mata run across to support (in between the midfield and defensive line).

Now we can see great combination play between 4 Spanish players.

First Ramos passes to Riera and he (because he is under pressure from behind) passes first time back to Negredo.

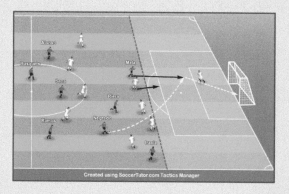

Negredo receives the ball in space and can see the space available on the weak side of the opposition. Mata is in a dangerous area where there is just 1 defender.

Negredo produces an excellent technical pass with the outside of his left foot in behind the defensive line and into the penalty area.

Mata runs quickly into the space faster than the defender and the goalkeeper. With 1 touch he scores the goal.

GOAL ANALYSIS

Attacking Combination Play: Maintaining Possession Before Quickly Switching Play to the Opposition's Weak Side (2)

11-Oct-2011: World Cup 2012 Qualifying

Spain 3-1 Scotland (3rd Goal): Villa - Assist: Silva

Spain in a 4-3-3 vs Scotland in a 4-4-2

Ramos is in an advanced position and Pique moves out wide. Busquets moves back into a centre back position and gets the ball (as if playing for Barca).

Spain then make a continuous series of short passes and when the defenders close them down, they immediately play the pass back.

Busquets passes to Pique, Pique to Silva, Silva passes back to Pique and Pique passes to Ramos on the right.

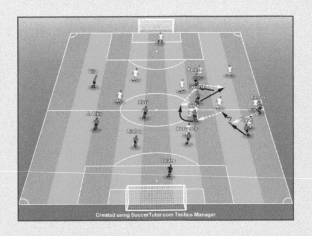

Ramos is under pressure from behind and cannot pass back because Pique has a player in front of him. Pique runs inside and provides a better supporting angle for Ramos and receives the pass.

Pique dribbles forward up to the opponent and passes inside to Silva.

Cazorla provides support and Silva plays a 1-2 combination with him before passing to Pedro.

Pedro passes to Cazorla who has moved to support him on the right.

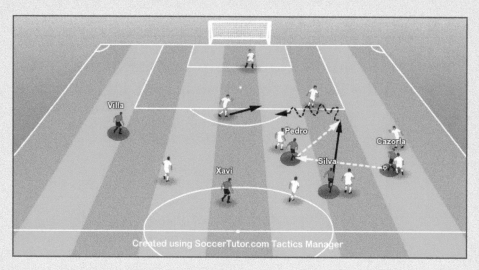

Now we see a third man run. Cazorla passes to Pedro again and while the ball is travelling to Pedro, Silva makes a run in between Cazorla and Pedro and receives the pass.

Silva shows good individual skill to change direction and beat the defender. He dribbles inside into the penalty area and the other defender moves to close him down.

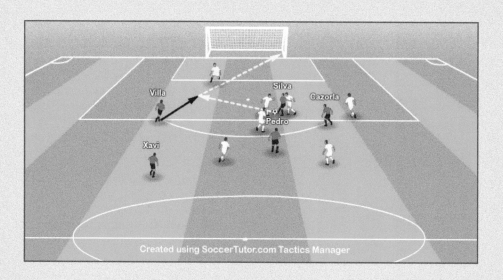

When Silva is closed down by the defender, he passes to Villa in space on the other side of the penalty area.

Villa is completely free after running from the other side and scores the goal.

SESSION FOR THIS TOPIC *(5 Practices)*

1. Attacking Combination with Change of Direction

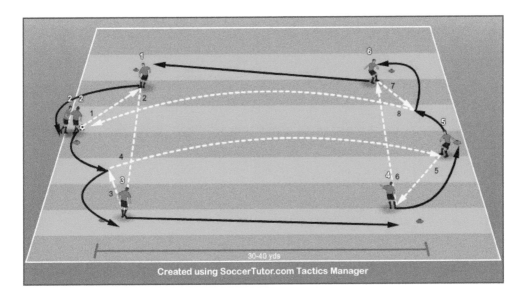

Objective

We work on a specific attacking combination pattern of play with a change of direction (switching play).

Description

We create 2 triangles with 30-40 yards distances between them. We work with 7 (or more) players with the starting positions shown in the diagram on in each triangle. The players are all limited to 1 touch.

The passing sequence starts with player 2 on one triangle who passes to player 1, player 1 passes to player 3 and player 3 passes back to player 2 who has moved to support. Player 2 plays a long pass to player 5 on the other triangle and changes the direction of the play.

Player 5 passes to player 4 who passes to player 6. Player 6 passes back to player 5 (who has moved to support) and player 5 plays a long pass to the next player in the player 2 position on the other side. The sequence is repeated and the practice continues the same way.

Each player moves onto the next position (1 to 2, 2 to 3 etc) including player 3 moving to the other side into player 4's position and player 6 moving across to player 1's position. You can also execute the same sequence running in the opposite direction.

Coaching Points

1. The practice must have a good rhythm, making sure the passes are timed to the movements.
2. Monitor the movement, angles and distances of support play.
3. Passes must be with the correct weight and be very accurate (to feet) throughout the practice.
4. Players should use 1 touch whenever possible throughout the entire exercise.
5. Both verbal and visual/optical communication is needed for the practice to run smoothly.

PROGRESSION
2. Attacking Combination with Change of Direction (2)

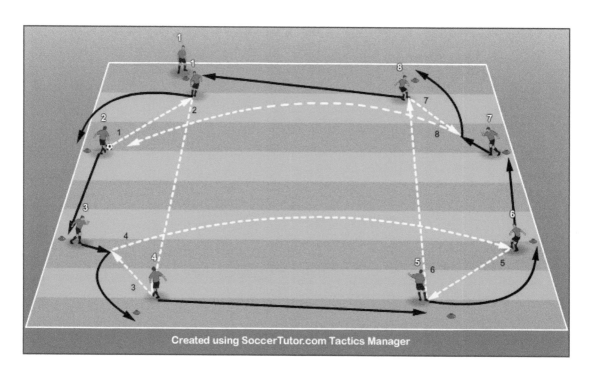

Created using SoccerTutor.com Tactics Manager

Description

We now have 4 positions on each side as shown in the diagram and work with 9 (or more) players. All players are limited to 1 touch again throughout the practice.

The passing sequence starts with player 2 who passes to player 1. Player 1 passes to player 4 who passes to Player 3. Player 3 plays a long ball to the other side (changing the point of attack) to player 6. Player 6 passes to player 5, player 5 passes to player 8 who passes back to player 7 (who moves to support). Player 7 plays a long ball to the other side to player 2 and the sequence continues in the same way.

Each player moves onto the next position (1 to 2, 2 to 3 etc) including player 4 moving to the other side into player 5's position and player 8 moving across to player 1's position. You can also execute the same sequence running in the opposite direction.

Coaching Points

1. The correct body shape should be monitored (opening up) and receiving/passing with the back foot (foot furthest away from the ball).
2. The practice should be executed with 1 touch whenever possible.

110

PROGRESSION
3. Attacking from the Back with One-Two Combinations Pattern of Play

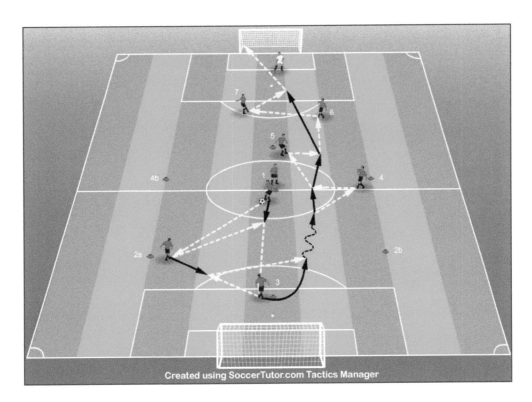

Created using SoccerTutor.com Tactics Manager

Objective
We work on a specific pattern of play to develop possession play with short passes and attacking combinations.

Description
Using a full pitch, we have 8 outfield players working on this pattern of play with one-two combinations. Player 1 starts with the ball in the centre and passes to player 2a. Player 2a passes back to him and player 1 passes to player 3. Player 3 passes to 2a who makes a supporting movement, before passing back to player 3 (out in front of him to run onto).

Player 3 dribbles forward and plays a 1-2 combination with both player 4 and player 5 (as shown). Player 3 then passes to player 6 who passes to player 7. While the pass to player 7 is travelling, player 3 makes a 3rd man run to receive the pass from player 7 into the box and shoots at goal.

Then run the practice with players positioned on 2b and 4b.

Coaching Point
Players should use 1 touch whenever possible to speed up play.

PROGRESSION

4. Switching Play & Attacking the Opposition's Weak Side in a Position Specific Attacking Combination Practice

PART 1

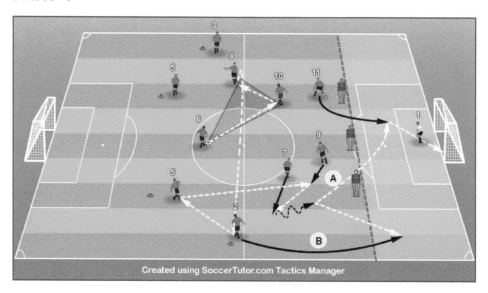

PART 2

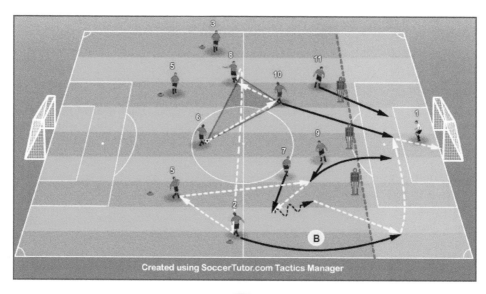

Objective

We work on short passes to keep possession in midfield, switching play and finishing the attack on the opposition's weak side quickly and efficiently.

Description

Now we work with players in specific positions to train tactical movements and combinations in a 4-3-3 formation or 4-1-4-1.

We have a combination between the 3 midfielders (6, 8 & 10) before No.8 plays a long pass to change the point of attack to the other full back. The right back (2) in the diagram example passes back to the centre back and immediately the right forward and the striker support him at different angles.

The centre back then passes forward to the striker (9), who passes back to the right forward (7) who has 2 options to pass beyond the defensive line. The most difficult option (but more creativity and better for the team) is to pass into the penalty area and in behind the defensive line (mannequins) to the left forward (11).

The second option is to pass into the space on the right flank for the advanced full back. If No.7 passes to him, the striker (9) makes a run to the near post and No.11 makes a run to the far post. No.10 will also make a run from behind and all other players run up to support the attack and close the distances between the lines.

Coaching Points

1. You can decide which players you want to go to the near or far post, and who runs up from behind (e.g. No.11 can go to the near post and No.9 to the far post).

2. Encourage the players to take the first option as it finishes the attack much more quickly and the defenders will be running back, facing their own goal. This makes the cross much more difficult to defend.

3. The second option will allow the defenders more time to get into a good position for the cross from the right back. The weak side of the opposition needs to be exploited quickly before the advantage is over.

PROGRESSION

5. Switching Play & Attacking the Opposition's Weak Side in a 4 Zone Game on a Full Pitch

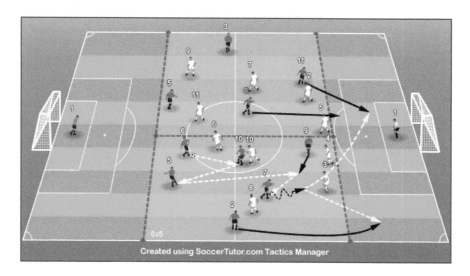

Description

Using a full pitch we create a middle zone and split it into 2 grids (left and right) as shown in the diagram. The red team are in a 4-3-3 or 4-1-4-1 and the white team are in a 4-4-2 or 4-2-3-1.

The game always starts with the red goalkeeper and the red team try to attack with good combination play within one grid. In a grid we always have a 6v5 numerical advantage for the reds (as shown in the diagram).

The other 4 red players are in the other grid. The second white centre back is positioned on the line between the 2 grids and the other 4 white players are in the other grid.

If the reds transfer the ball from one side to the other, they must then create the same numerical situation (6v5 again). The point of the game is for the red team to attack using the same combination play on one side using the 2 options we worked on in the previous practice:

1. After some combination play with short passes, switch the play and cross the ball early into the other attacker (11 - on the other side) inside the penalty area.
2. The second is to attack using the full back's advanced run.

If the whites win the ball, they go into transition to attack and must finish their attack within 10 seconds. This rule forces the red team to move very quickly from attack to defence when they lose the ball.

Rules

1. Before being able to use an attacking solution in one zone, the team must complete 6 passes in there (if team switch play to other side, 6 new passes must be made in that grid before an attack is allowed there).
2. The white players can only defend within their own grid.
3. The red players are limited to 2-3 touches in the beginning and 1-2 touches as we progress.
4. The white team have unlimited touches.

GOAL ANALYSIS

Passing through the Midfield Line in the Centre (1)

26-Jun-2008: European Championship 2008 Semi Final

Spain 3-0 Russia (1st Goal): Xavi - Assist: Iniesta

Spain in a 4-4-2 vs Russia in a 4-1-3-2

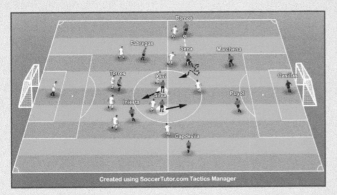

Spain are in possession against an organised defence in the middle zone.

Ramos passes inside to Senna who dribbles inside so he can find a solution to move the ball forward.

Xavi and Silva make opposite supporting movements. Silva comes deep and Xavi moves in behind the midfield line (and away from the 2 centre midfielders).

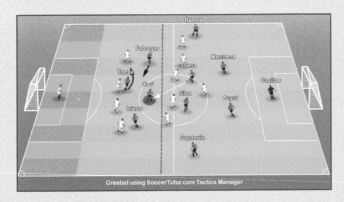

Senna passes forward to Xavi and takes 6 Russian players out of the game.

Xavi receives on the half turn and moves into the high zone. He has 4 Russian defenders in front of him and 3 teammates in a 4v4 situation for the attack.

Torres changes direction towards the right, Iniesta is on the left and Fabregas (moving from the right) supports Xavi inside.

SPAIN Attacking Sessions

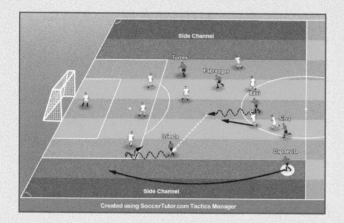

Xavi dribbles forward and is under pressure from behind, so passes to Iniesta on the left near the penalty area.

All players from both teams are within the width of the penalty area (as shown) and there is free space on both side channels (left and right).

Iniesta shows good control up against the right back and gives time to Capdevila to make an overlapping run into the space on the left side channel (2v1 situation).

Iniesta uses the run as a decoy, transferring the ball to his right foot and cuts inside.

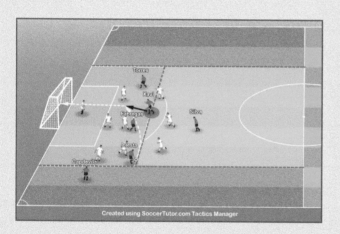

There are 2 Spanish players inside the box, but they are static (Fabregas and Torres).

A third player Xavi has run from deep and arrives in the penalty area.

Iniesta finds the right solution and makes a short and hard cross into the penalty area to Xavi, who with 1 touch volleys the ball into the net.

GOAL ANALYSIS
Passing through the Midfield Line in the Centre (2)
29-Jun-2008: European Championship 2008 Final

Spain 1-0 Germany: Torres - Assist: Xavi
Spain in a 4-1-4-1 vs Germany in a 4-2-3-1

Spain play continuous passes forcing the German team (who have a very good defensive organisation in a 4-2-3- 1 in the middle zone) to make consecutive runs and sideways movements.

Spain try to find solutions to pass the ball through the lines. Also, the Spanish players make continuous support movements, both around the ball zone and further away into space.

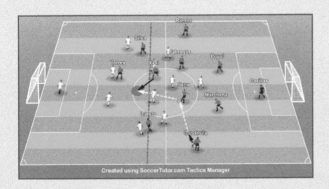

The ball is moved to Capdevila on the left and he pass inside to Senna. At this moment, Xavi moves in behind the 2 centre midfielders and the majority of the German team.

Senna passes the ball forward in between the 2 centre midfielders to Xavi.

Now Xavi has the 2-3-1 part of Germany's formation behind him and only 3 defenders in front of him.

SPAIN Attacking Sessions

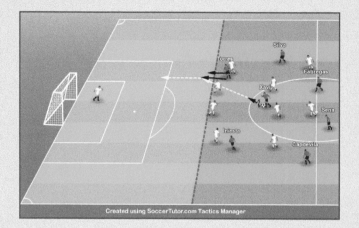

Xavi takes an excellent directional first touch and turns. With his second touch he makes a quality pass into the space in between the left back and the left centre back.

Torres has made the run and has an advantage with his better starting position compared to the centre back who is static.

Torres runs through and is in a 1v1 situation with the left back.

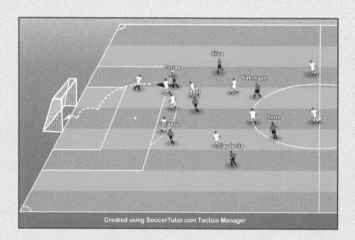

Torres is accomplished to get to the ball first and wins the race with the left back and the goalkeeper.

Torres finishes with a little chip over the goalkeeper who goes to ground.

The goal was very well converted under pressure of time and space.

SESSION FOR THIS TOPIC *(5 Practices)*

1. 10 v 10 Passing through the Lines in a 6 Zone Possession Game

Created using SoccerTutor.com Tactics Manager

Objective

To develop quick combination play with a focus on passing forward through the lines.

Description

In an area 36 x 20 yards we mark out 6 zones (6 x 20 yards each). We work with 2 teams of 10 players and each team has 3 zones with players positioned inside. They each have 2 players at the back and both have 4 players in another 2 zones. All players stay within their zone, except for the 2 players from both teams in the 'safe zones' who can move forward into the next one.

The game starts in an end zone with one team in possession and the objective is to play forward through the lines across their 3 zones and back again. If the other team wins the ball, they have the exact same aim.

Different Rules

1. All players are limited to 2 or 3 touches.
2. All players are limited to 1 touch and 2 touches if they win the ball from their opponents.
3. For each pass from one grid to another, the team scores 1 point.
4. If one team can be transfer the ball between their 3 zones and then back again, they score an extra 2 points.

PROGRESSION

2. Passing through the Lines in a 3 Zone Possession Game with a Middle Safety Zone

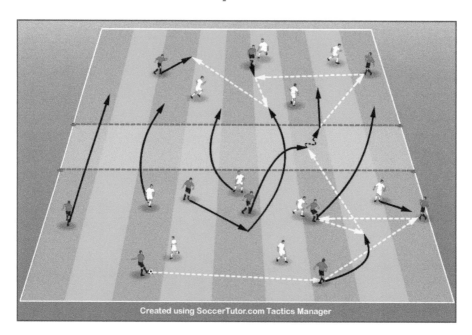

Created using SoccerTutor.com Tactics Manager

Description

In an area 65 x 45 yards we mark out 3 zones. The 2 end zones are 30 x 45 yards and the central zone (safe zone for the team in possession) is 5 x 50 yards. We play a 10v10 game.

The drill starts with one team in possession (reds in diagram). Within this first zone we have a 7v6 situation.

The reds (team in possession) are in a 4-3 formation and the whites (defending) are in a 4-2 formation. In the other grid we have a 3v4 situation.

The objective for the 7 reds is to pass the ball into the central zone (safe zone, no marking allowed) and one of the 3 midfielders makes a run to receive. If this happens, they then pass to the other grid and run across to support the 3 teammates, Another 3 red players and 2 whites also run across from the first zone to create the same 7v6 situation again. The objective is exactly the same.

If the white team win the ball, the roles changes and they must create the same 7v6 numerical situation.

Different Rules

1. All players have unlimited touches (or 3 touches).
2. All players have unlimited touches (or 3 touches), except the player who receives the ball in the safe zone is limited to 2 touches in there.

Coaching Points

1. Players need to move from one zone to the other very quickly to provide support (passing options).
2. The pass into the safe zone needs to be with the correct weight and timed for a teammate's run forward.

PROGRESSION
3. Passing through the Midfield Line in the Centre in a Position Specific Zonal Game

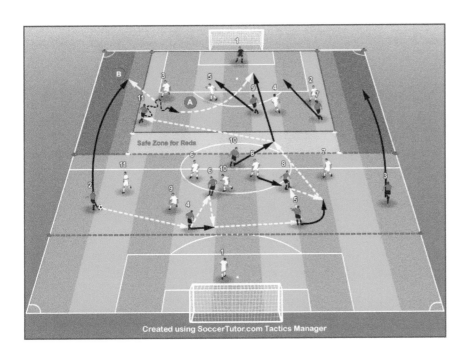

Objective

We work on the specific attacking combination used for Xavi's goal against Russia shown in the analysis.

Description

We split a full pitch into 6 zones as shown in the diagram (the high zone is split in 4 - the centre, 2 side channels & a safe zone). In the middle zone we play 7v6 with the reds in a 4-3 formation and the whites in a 4-2 or 4-1-1.

The first objective for the reds is to pass the ball into the safe zone (behind the midfield line) where one of the 3 red midfielders will receive. If this happens, that player is limited to 2 touches to pass to a teammate in the high zone (there is a 3v4 situation there) and runs forward to support. The 2 full backs can also run up to support the attackers and give them an extra solution out wide (in the side channels).

The left or right forward has 2 options/solutions in the high zone:

A) Pass in behind the back 4 into the penalty area for the run of the midfielder or the 2 other attackers.
B) Pass to the full back out wide. The full back is limited to 2 touches in the side zones.

If the white team win the ball at anytime, all white players are free to move across all zones and they try to score in the opposite goal. The reds must move quickly from attack to defence (negative transition).

Rules

1. The red players in the low zone have unlimited touches, but the midfielder in the safe zone is always limited to 2 touches.
2. The red players in the high zone should have limited touches (coach's discretion).
3. In the transition to defence, red defenders are not allowed inside the low zone before the ball is played in there.

PROGRESSION

4. Passing through the Midfield Line in the Centre in a Position Specific Zonal Game (2)

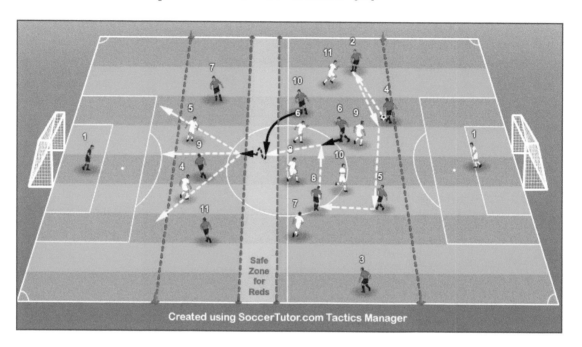

Created using SoccerTutor.com Tactics Manager

Objective

We work on the specific attacking combination used for the Torres goal against Germany shown in the analysis.

Description

We split a full pitch into 5 zones but differently this time (see diagram). We have a low zone (safe zone for attacking) and a zone in front of it where we have a 7v6 situation with the reds in a 4-3 formation and the whites in a 2-3-1 formation.

The first objective for the reds is to pass the ball into the safe zone (behind the midfield line) where one of the 3 red midfielders will receive. If this happens, that player is limited to 2 touches to pass to a teammate in the high zone (there is a 3v4 situation there) and runs forward to support.

In the high zone we have 3 attackers vs 2 centre backs. The defenders play fully active defence after the pass of the midfielder.

The midfielder has 3 passing options; he has 2 options out wide on the outside of the defenders and the third is to pass in between the 2 centre backs for the striker's run. All options are in behind the defensive line.

Whatever option the midfielder takes, he runs forward into the penalty area (to support) after making the pass.

If the white team win the ball at anytime, all white players are free to move across all zones and they try to score in the opposite goal. The reds must move quickly from attack to defence (negative transition).

PROGRESSION

5. Passing through the Midfield Line in the Centre in a Position Specific Zonal Game (3)

Created using SoccerTutor.com Tactics Manager

Objective

We work on the specific attacking combination used for the Torres goal against Germany shown in the analysis.

Description

In this progression we simply add the 2 full backs for the white team. This makes it harder for the reds team to score as we now have a 4v4 situation in the high zone. All the other instructions/rules stay the same.

If the white team win the ball at anytime, all white players are free to move across all zones and they try to score in the opposite goal. The reds must move quickly from attack to defence (negative transition).

Coaching Points

1. This practice trains passing through an opposition set up with a 4-2-3-1 formation specifically, but you can adapt either team to whichever formation you would like.

2. The safety zone works very well to get the players used to receiving in behind the midfield line in space.

3. The attack in the final third (4v4) should be finished quickly with quality passing, movement and finishing.

SPAIN Attacking Sessions

GOAL ANALYSIS

Passing through the Midfield Line on the Flank

23-Jun-2012: European Championship 2012 Quarter Final

Spain 2-0 France (1st Goal): Alonso - Assist: J. Alba

Spain in a 4-2-3-1 vs France in a 4-1-4-1

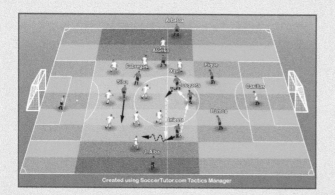

All Spain's players from the 4-2-3-1 (except the full backs) are in the centre of the pitch. They keep possession and create a numerical superiority around the ball with continuous supporting movements for the ball carrier.

The 2 full backs are available out wide. Iniesta, Busquets and Xavi move the ball from left to right and back again. When Iniesta has the opportunity and the space, he dribbles the ball forward on the left.

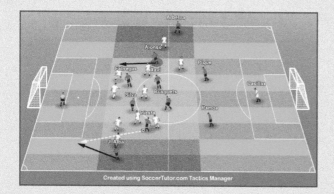

This creates an opportunity for Spain on the left with Iniesta and Alba in a 2v1 situation against the right back.

J.Alba quickly changes speed and accelerates, asking for the ball in the space behind the back 4 (in between the right back and the centre back).

Other players move forward to make supporting runs and Alonso makes a good run on the other side (weak side of the opposition in this attack).

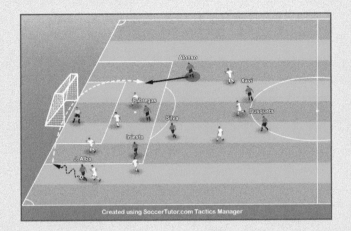

Alba has a speed advantage and beats the left back, then dribbles to the byline. 3 players (Iniesta, Fabregas and Silva) run to support him in the penalty area where there are 3 defenders.

At the correct time, Alonso runs in from the other side to the far post and Alba recognises the situation.

Alba crosses the ball to the far post where Alonso is left unmarked.

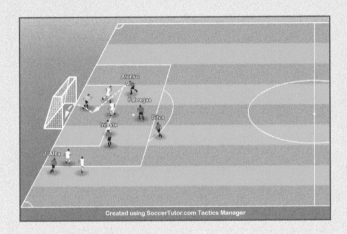

Alonso scores with a downwards header into the far corner and makes it 1-0 to Spain.

SESSION FOR THIS TOPIC *(3 Practices)*

1. 6 v 6 (+6) Position Specific 5 Zone Possession Game

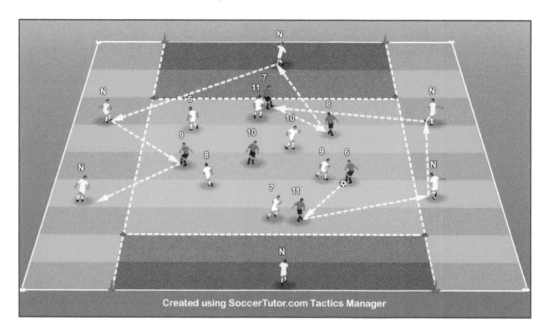

Created using SoccerTutor.com Tactics Manager

Objective
To develop quick combination play with a focus on passing the ball out wide and keeping possession.

Description
In an area 45 x 35 yards we create 4 zones as shown in the diagram. The central zone is 35 x 25 yards, the 2 side zones are 35 x 5 yards and the 2 end zones are 5 x 35 yards.

In the central zone have a 6v6 situation with both teams in a 2-3-1 formation. There is 1 neutral player on each side and 2 neutral players at the top and bottom. The side neutrals can be the full backs and the end neutrals can be the centre backs from the 4-2-3-1.

The objective is to maintain possession in a 6 (+6) v 6 game using the neutral players to work the ball from end to end. If a team completes 8 passes they score 1 point and if they keep the ball for 30 seconds they score 2 points.

If the defending team wins the ball, the teams change roles and they have exactly the same objectives.

Different Rules
1. The neutrals can pass to each other, but these passes do not count as part of completing 8 to get a point.
2. The neutrals are not allowed to exchange 3 consecutive passes.
3. The inside players have unlimited touches and the neutrals are limited to 1-2 touches.
4. The inside players are limited to 3 touches and the neutrals have 1-2 touches.
5. The inside players are limited to 2 touches and the neutrals have 1 touch.
6. All players are limited to 1 touch.

PROGRESSION
2. 10 v 10 Position Specific 5 Zone Possession Game

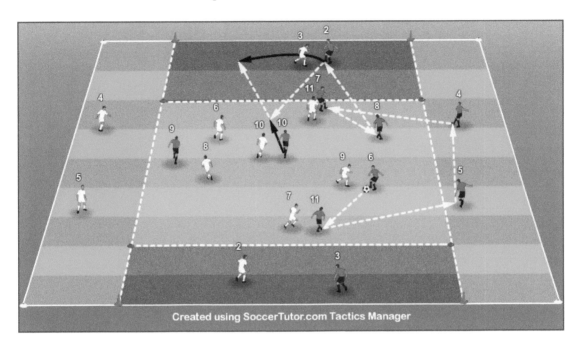

Created using SoccerTutor.com Tactics Manager

Description

For this progression we now replace the neutral players with full backs and centre backs for both teams. This makes it much more difficult to keep possession and score points.

The same objectives and rules from the previous practice apply again (neutral player rules are applied to the full backs and centre backs on the outsides).

Coaching Points

1. The correct body shape should be monitored (opening up) and receiving/passing with the back foot (foot furthest away from the ball).
2. Players should vary their passes - passes to feet and passes into space.
3. The correct angles and distances for support play are required and should be monitored.
4. Players need to demonstrate good awareness and quick decision making to maintain possession under pressure.
5. Collective pressing (with good defensive shape) is key to trying to win the ball from the opposition.

PROGRESSION

3. Passing through the Midfield Line on the Flanks in a Position Specific 5 Zone Game

A

B

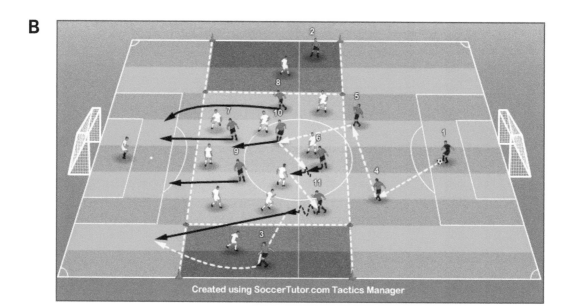

Objective

We work on keeping possession in the centre and passing to an advanced full back on the flank to get in behind the midfield and defensive lines.

Description

We use a full pitch now and create a middle attacking zone divided into 3 zones (1 central and 2 side zones). The red team are in a 4-2-3-1 formation and the white team are in a 4-1-4-1. We play a normal 11v11 game.

The focus for the red team is to attack using the flanks (although they can also attack from the centre).

They keep possession in the central zone and wait for the correct time to attack. The full backs are positioned in the side zones and they are the only ones allowed to play in there (except for a wide forward's run in a one-two combination with the full back - solution 2).

The diagrams show 2 solutions which we should work on to attack using the flank in this game. The first is a pass out wide to the full back who crosses into the penalty area.

The second shows the wide forward passing to the full back and then making a diagonal cutting run in front of the full back. This creates a 2v1 numerical superiority on the flank and the full back passes the ball down the line for the wide forward (No.11 in diagram) to receive in an advanced position on the flank and then cross into the penalty area.

If the whites win the ball, they must finish their counter attack within 10-12 seconds.

Rules

1. If the red team score by attacking through the centre, they score 1 point and if they score with an attack from the flank they score 2 points.
2. If the whites score within 10-12 seconds of winning the ball, they get 2 points.

GOAL ANALYSIS

Attacking in Behind the Defensive Line (1)

14-Oct-2009: World Cup 2010 Qualifying

Bosnia Hz 2-5 Spain (4th Goal): Silva - Assist: Negredo

Spain in a 4-1-4-1 vs Bosnia Hz in a 4-1-3-2

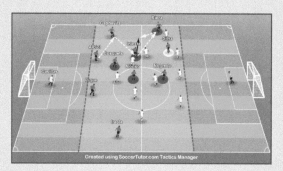

Spain are up against an opponent which defends in the middle zone and keep small distances between the lines.

Spain are in a 4-1-4-1 and most of their players are on 1 side (left in this situation) and the width on the other side is provided only by the right back (Iraola).

The midfielders and striker are all positioned in and around the ball zone, but in different lines to provide multiple solutions for their possession game.

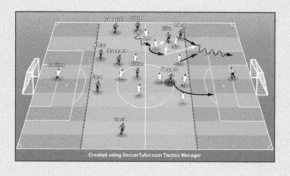

After exchanging many passes, Iniesta receives on the left and starts the attack. The first step is against the midfield line. Iniesta dribbles past the right midfielder and plays a 1-2 combination with Silva which takes a centre midfielder out of the game.

Iniesta now only has 4 defenders in front of him and there is a lot of free space in behind them. Riera and Iniesta recognise the situation and cooperate. Iniesta passes in between the right back and the centre back, Riera receives in behind and dribbles into the box.

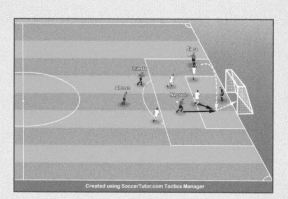

Now all players (both attackers and defenders) are running facing the goal.

Riera passes across the box and behind the defenders to the back post.

Negredo wins the battle with the centre back and scores the goal.

GOAL ANALYSIS

Attacking in Behind the Defensive Line (2)

29-Mar-2011: European Championship 2012 Qualifying

Lithuania 1-3 Spain (2nd Goal): Own goal - Assist: Mata

Spain in a 4-1-4-1

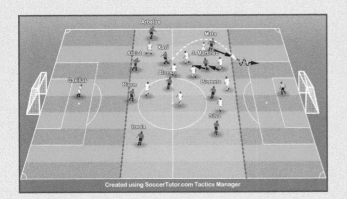

Spain are again up against a defensive organisation in the middle zone with good distances, but without good pressure on the ball carrier. Xavi has the ball, J. Martinez comes short to support and the defender follows him.

Xavi is in possession and has the space to make a technical lofted ball in behind the back 4. Mata is running into the space and Xavi's pass eliminates the defensive organisation. Mata receives ahead of the defenders and dribbles into the box.

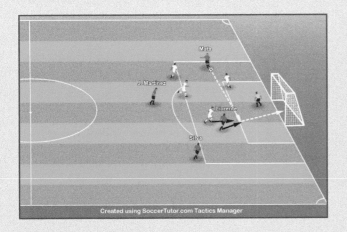

One defender runs back but there is a distance between him and Mata who has space to make the short cross to the back post.

Llorente has made a run from deep to the back post. The defender and Llorente are both facing the goal.

Under pressure from Llorente, the ball hits the defender and he scores an own goal.

SPAIN Attacking Sessions

GOAL ANALYSIS
Attacking in Behind the Defensive Line (3)
01-Jul-2012: European Championship 2012 Final
Spain 4-0 Italy (2nd Goal): J. Alba - Assist: Xavi
Spain in a 4-2-3-1 vs Italy in a 4-4-2 (Diamond Midfield)

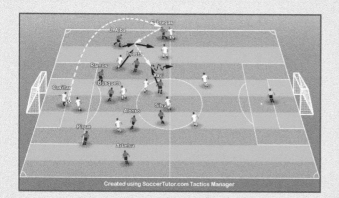

Casillas is pressed by the opposition attacker and has no short passing options. He plays a long ball to the left side of the pitch towards Fabregas.

Fabregas is under pressure from behind and heads back to Alba.

J. Alba is very quick and gets to the ball before the opponent and passes inside to Xavi, before running up the pitch himself to support.

The Italian midfield line is unbalanced and the defence are static. J. Alba makes a very fast run to support Xavi and goes in behind the defensive line.

Xavi recognises the situation and plays an excellent pass into to the space at the exact right time.

J. Alba now has the advantage against the Italian defenders, takes a good first touch out in front and with his second touch he scores the second goal of the Final.

SESSION FOR THIS TOPIC *(5 Practices)*

1. Attacking in Behind the Defensive Line in an 8 v 8 (+4) 2 Zone Possession Game

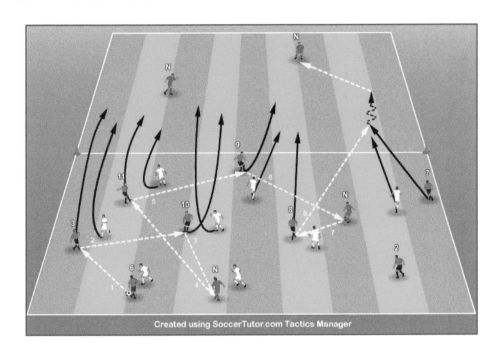

Created using SoccerTutor.com Tactics Manager

Objective

We develop possession play with the focus on passing in behind the defensive line.

Description

In an area 60 x 40 yards, we divide the pitch into 2 zones (30 x 40 yards each). We have 2 teams of 8 and 2 neutrals in each zone. The 8 players are in a 2-3-3 (with 2 full backs) the 4-3-3 formation.

The objective for the team in possession is to complete 6-8 passes and then transfer the ball to the other zone (in behind the defensive line) to a teammate who runs forward to receive. All players (except the 2 neutrals) then move across to the other zone and have the same objective.

We have 2 options once the ball is transferred to the other zone: 1) The new count of passes starts straight away (1,2,3.. to complete 6-8 passes) or 2) The count starts once every player from the team in possession has run into the second zone.

If the defenders win the ball at any time, the teams change roles. Each time the ball is transferred from one zone to the other, that team scores 1 point.

Different Rules

1. All players have unlimited touches (or 3 touches) and neutrals have 2 touches.
2. All players are limited to 2 touches and neutrals have 1 touch.

133

PROGRESSION
2. Attacking in Behind the Defensive Line in an 8 v 8 2 Zone Possession Game with 4 Goals

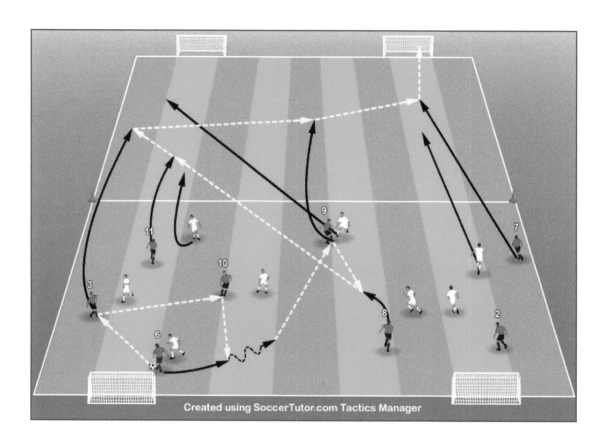

Created using SoccerTutor.com Tactics Manager

Objective

The same as the previous drill, but now we also develop accurate finishing.

Description

In this progression we add 4 mini goals (2 at each end) and remove the neutral players. We start in one zone and one team starts with the ball and attacks. The other team defends.

The objective for the team in possession is to move the ball in behind the defensive line and score in one of the 2 mini goals in the other zone. They pass the ball past the defenders to the other zone (in behind the defensive line) to a teammate who runs forward to receive.

If the defending team win the ball at any time, they must counter attack (try to score within same grid) and finish within 6-8 seconds. In either case, when the attack is finished or the ball goes out of play, the drill continues from the other zone and with the other team starting a new attack.

134

PROGRESSION
3. Attacking in Behind the Defensive Line in an 8 v 8 Game with 2 Goals

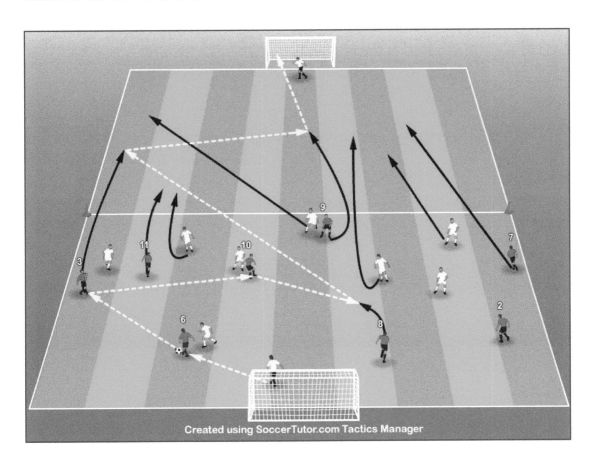

Created using SoccerTutor.com Tactics Manager

Objective
The same as the previous drill, but now we also train shooting/finishing against a goalkeeper in a full sized goal.

Description
The only difference in this progression is we replace the mini goals with 2 full sized goals with goalkeepers.

Coaching Points
1. Players should use different types of passes - short passes to feet and medium/long passes into space.
2. The final ball needs to be with the correct weight and timed well with the run into the second zone.
3. Players should use 1 touch whenever possible throughout the practice to attack quickly.
4. The players should finish with 1 touch to practice being under pressure of time and space.
5. There should be very quick runs into the high zone (good support play).

135

PROGRESSION

4. Attacking in Behind the Defensive Line in a 9 v 9 (+2) 3 Zone Game

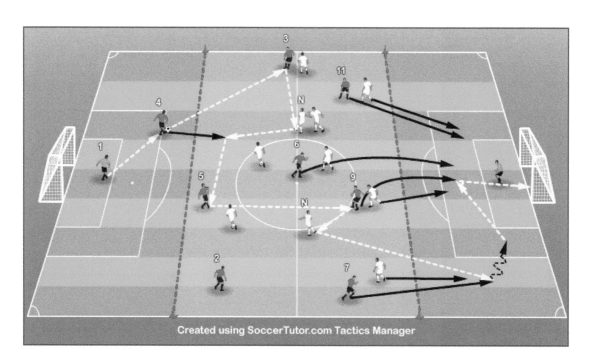

Created using SoccerTutor.com Tactics Manager

Objective

We develop possession play with the focus on passing in behind the defensive line, crossing and finishing.

Description

Using a full pitch we create a middle zone and play 8v8 (+2 neutral players) within it with one team starting in possession (from the goalkeeper). The formation for the team in possession can be 2-3-3 or 3-2-3.

Both of the 2 neutral players must touch the ball before any players from the team in possession are allowed to leave the zone and finish their attack in the final third. The defenders are allowed to leave the zone once an attacking player does.

If the defending team win the ball at any time, the teams change roles. They then have to keep possession and both neutral players have to touch the ball before they can attack.

PROGRESSION

5. Attacking in Behind the Defensive Line in an 11 v 11 3 Zone Game

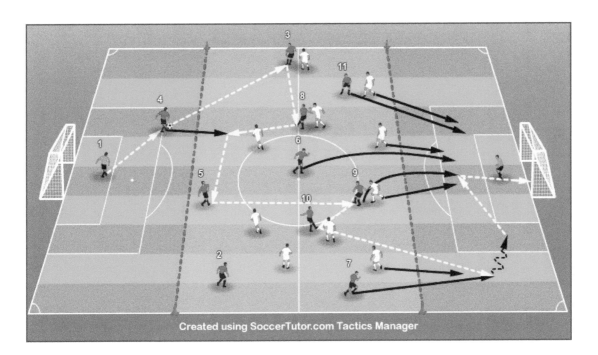

Created using SoccerTutor.com Tactics Manager

Description

The difference in this progression is that we now play an 11v11 game and remove the neutral players completely.

The red team are in a 4-3-3 formation and the white team are in a 4-2-3-1.

CHAPTER 3

Attacking Against Teams which Defend in the High Zone

Attacking Against Teams which Defend in the High Zone

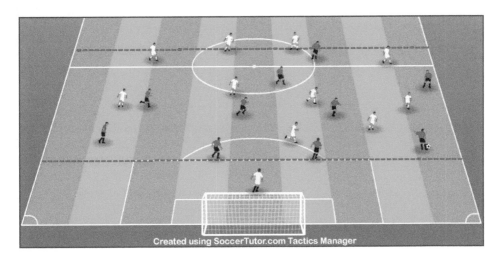

Created using SoccerTutor.com Tactics Manager

Only 2 out of Spain's 86 goals (2008-2012) were scored attacking against teams which defended in the high zone.

Very few teams defended against Spain in the high zone. All Spain's opponents (even the best teams in the world) focused their defensive organisation in the middle zone or the low zone.

The 2 goals in this situation were from 2008 and 2009. The first goal was against Russia in the Semi Final at Euro 2008 when Spain were leading 2-0 and Russia pushed players forward to try and get back into the game. The other was the 4th goal against Belgium in a comfortable 5-0 victory in a World Cup qualifying game.

Situation 1

Spain had good possession with continuous short passes to feet and many supporting movements for the ball carrier. This attracted the opposition into one area and Spain suddenly change the rhythm of play with a long pass to eliminate the defensive block and get in behind the defensive line quickly.

Spain launch a fast attack when the opposition are unbalanced and have space in behind their defence. The quality of the Spanish team (as individuals and as a group) makes the difference in this situation.

Situation 2

This was the same as situation 1 with only 1 difference. Once the opposition are drawn into one area, Spain switch the point of attack from one side to the other.

They attack the weak side of the opposition and go in behind the defence again.

GOAL ANALYSIS

Building Up Play Against Opponents who Press High Up the Pitch (1)

26-Jun-2008: European Championship 2008 Semi Final

Spain 3-0 Russia (3rd Goal): Silva - Assist: Fabregas

Spain in a 4-4-2 vs Russia in a 4-1-3-2

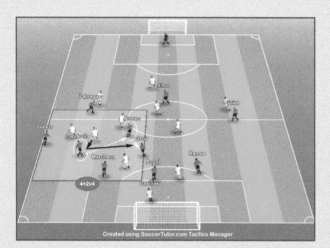

70 minutes gone, Russia are losing 2-0 and change their formation to 3-4-1-2 and try to press in the high zone. Spain display good movement/angles and distances to support the player with the ball to keep possession.

In this case 4 Russians try to press the ball on Spain's left side in the low zone. Iniesta is on the left flank and Senna is to the right (inside) providing support.

Fabregas is at the top and Marchena behind gives length support. Capdevila passes to Alonso who moved inside. Spain build a 4 (+2) v 4 situation (like a rondo game).

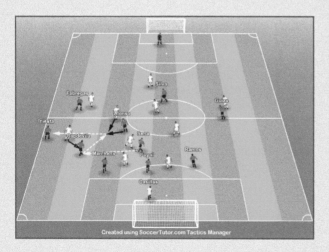

Capdevila and Alonso take up good positions and provide good angles and distances of support.

Senna passes to Capdevila. He is under pressure from his opponent and passes first time to Alonso who provides good support.

Alonso is also under pressure and now Iniesta is the free player who receives the pass from Alonso at the side.

So with the 4 (+2) v 4 situation, the Spanish players keep the ball and break through the pressure of the opposition.

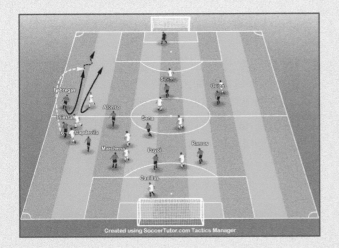

Now after the series of passing, Iniesta has time and space. He shows good cooperation with good synchronisation with Fabregas at the top.

Fabregas makes a checking away movement and runs in behind the defensive line high up on the right flank. Iniesta plays the pass down the line into the space.

Silva and Guiza also move forward from the centre and the right respectively to support him.

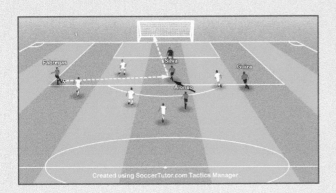

Fabregas receives the ball and dribbles into the penalty area and at the correct time, passes to Silva who has run from the back.

Silva takes a good first touch and finishes very well to score the third goal for Spain.

SESSION FOR THIS TOPIC *(5 Practices)*

1. Possession Play & Pressing in a 6 v 4 Transition Game

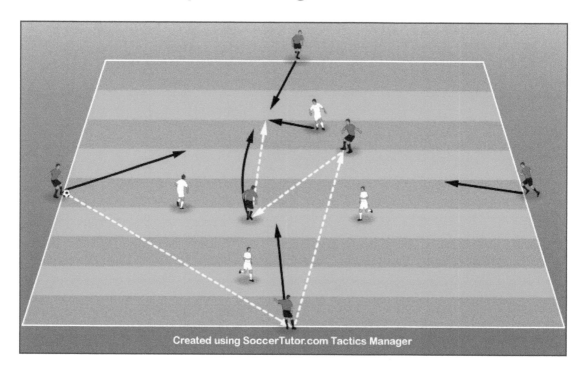

Created using SoccerTutor.com Tactics Manager

Objective

We work on keeping possession and immediate pressing when the ball is lost (to close the time and space).

Description

In an area 18 x 12 yards we work with 10 players. The reds have 6 players and the whites have 4 players. The red team have 4 players on the sides of the grid and 2 players inside.

At the bottom and at the top we put centre backs and attacking midfielders (or attackers) and at the sides we have full backs (or wide midfielders/forwards). The 2 red inside players are centre midfielders. The white team of 4 has all their players inside the grid (use centre midfielders).

The objective for the red team is to keep possession and if they lose the ball, all 6 players move in and make a quick transition to defence and try to win the ball back immediately. The white team try and keep possession.

When the reds have the ball they are OPEN (spread out in space at good angles) and when they lose the ball they CLOSE (move in and around the ball zone).

Rules

1. The red players are limited to 2 touches and the white players have unlimited touches.
2. If the reds complete 8-10 passes they get 1 point and if they keep possession for 30 seconds they get 2 points.
3. If the whites win the ball and complete 4-5 passes or keep the ball for 6 seconds they get 1 point.

VARIATION
2. Transition to Defence / Attack in a 4 (+2) v 4 Possession Game

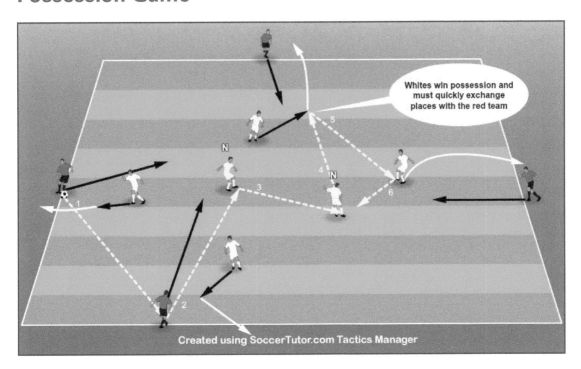

Whites win possession and must quickly exchange places with the red team

Created using SoccerTutor.com Tactics Manager

Description

Within the same area we have 2 teams of 4 and 2 extra neutral players who always play within the grid and with the team which has possession of the ball.

The team which starts in possession has all their players at the sides, the other team's players are all inside along with the 2 neutral players (yellow).

The first objective is the same as the previous practice, but now when the defending team win the ball, both teams change roles and make a transition from attack to defence and vice versa.

Rules

1. All players are limited to 2 touches.
2. The neutral players are limited to 1 touch.

Coaching Points

1. The correct angles/distances of support and verbal/optical communication should be monitored.
2. In tight spaces, the accuracy of the short passes is key to maintaining possession.
3. The correct body shape should be monitored (opening up) and receiving/passing with the back foot (foot furthest away from the ball).
4. This practice tests the players reactions to a changing game situation (transition to defence or attack).

143

PROGRESSION

3. Attacking from the Back & Quickly Providing Support in a 2 Zone Possession Game

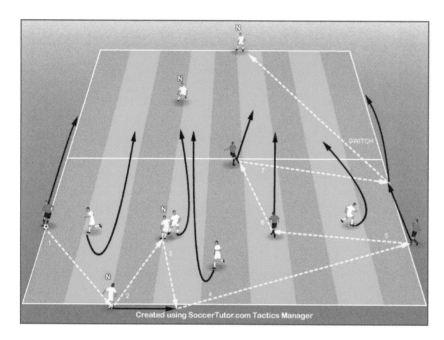

Objective

To develop possession play, while focusing specifically on passing the ball forwards quickly from the back and providing fast support.

Description

We now have 2 grids (18 x 12 yards each) and work with 12 players. There are 2 teams of 4 and 4 extra neutrals.

The practice starts in one grid and the reds have possession as shown in the diagram. There is 1 neutral at the bottom and 1 inside the grid. There are 3 red players on the sides and 1 inside so we have a 6 v 4 situation. The 2 other neutral players are waiting in the other grid (1 at the top and 1 inside).

The objective for the team in possession is to complete 6-8 passes in one grid and then pass the ball to the other grid. If this happens all players (except the 2 neutrals) must move across and the drill continues the same way, trying to complete 6-8 passes again before moving back to the first grid.

If the defending team (white in diagram) win the ball they have 2 options:

1. They must complete 6-8 passes in the same grid they win the ball in before moving to the other one.
2. Progress to them passing immediately to the other grid and moving quickly across to start their possession.

Rules

1. All players are limited to 2 touches.
2. All red and white players are limited to 2 touches and the neutral players have 1 touch.

PROGRESSION

4. Attacking from the Back Under Pressure in a 6 v 5 Dynamic Game

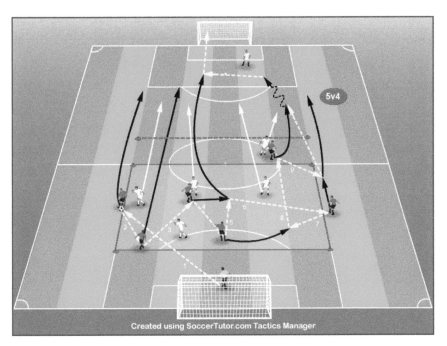

Created using SoccerTutor.com Tactics Manager

Description

We now use a full pitch. We create a zone in the area shown in the diagram. Inside the square, we have the same 6v4 situation again and we also have 1 defender in an extra area between the halfway line and a marked out line we create (8 yards past halfway line). There are goalkeepers in full sized goals for both teams.

The game starts with the red goalkeeper who passes into the square and the red team's objective is to keep possession and complete 8 passes. After this and when there is an opening, they launch a fast attack with 5 reds vs 4 whites. There should be a pass for the attacker in behind the marked out line and then all players (except 1 red player who stays in the square) move to support and attack using the full half of the pitch.

If the white team win the ball within the square, they try to score in the other goal and the red team must make a fast transition from attack to defence. If the reds win the ball back again, they must move the ball back into the zone again and complete 8 passes before launching another fast attack.

Different Rules

1. All players are limited to 2-3 touches.
2. Red outside players have 1 touch and the inside players have 2-3 touches.
3. Red outside players have 2-3 touches and the inside players have 1 touch.
4. Players have unlimited touches in the high zone.
5. The white players have 6 seconds from the moment they win the ball to finish their attack.
6. The white defender at the back is passive / The white defender at the back is fully active.

145

PROGRESSION

5. Attacking from the Back in a Dynamic Zonal Attacking Game

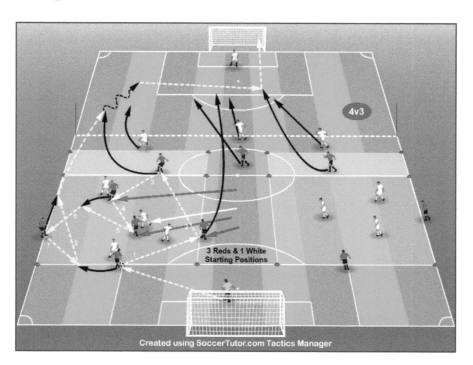

Description

In this progression we create 2 zones with 1 zone at either side of the pitch as shown in the diagram. The zones are 24 x 24 yards and have an additional smaller zone which is 6 x 24 yards. We also create a line from one sideline to the other, which is 12 yards beyond the halfway line.

There are 10 red players, 10 white players and 2 goalkeepers. The starting positions are as follows: 3 outside reds and 3 inside whites positioned in each zone, 3 red players + 1 white player standing in between the 2 zones and 1 red attacker in the centre of the pitch with 3 white defenders behind him.

The practice starts with the red goalkeeper who passes to a teammate in one of the 2 zones and the 3 reds & 1 white player in between the zones quickly move there (left zone in diagram).

The reds aim to keep possession in one grid under pressure from the whites. If they complete 8 passes they can then go into a fast attack with 4 reds vs 3 white (2 red players from that zone including the player at the top, the player at the top of the other zone and the red attacker in the centre play against the 3 white defenders).

If the whites win the ball, they attack the opposite goal and if they score it counts double. This rule helps the red team to move quickly from attack into a transition to defence. (Win the ball - OPEN, lose the ball - CLOSED). If the reds win the ball back, they take up their original positions and the practice restarts with the goalkeeper.

Rule

All the different rules on the limit of touches from the previous practice can be applied.

GOAL ANALYSIS

Building Up Play Against Opponents who Press High Up the Pitch (2)

05-Sep-2009: World Cup 2010 Qualifying

Spain 5-0 Belgium (4th Goal): Silva - Assist: Arbeloa

Spain in a 4-4-2 vs Belgium in a 4-2-3-1

Spain have a throw in deep in their own half on the left and Belgium press in the high zone.

Riera checks away from his opponent and Capdevila throws the ball to him and moves to provide immediate support.

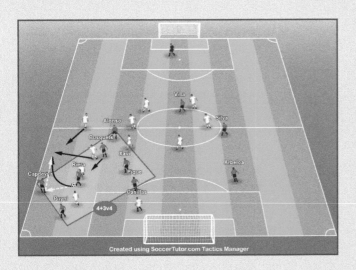

4 Belgium players press the ball but Spain are again able to keep possession in their own half with good movement and above all with good angles and distances to support the player with the ball.

Puyol is positioned at the bottom, Alonso at the top, Capdevila to the left and Pique to the right.

Riera, Busquets and Xavi are also inside the marked zone and build a 4 (+3) v 4 situation (like a rondo possession game).

SPAIN Attacking Sessions

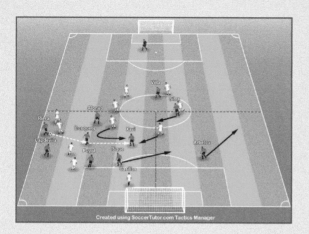

In this case Spain keep possession in the left half of the pitch and when the opponents are drawn into this area, they move to quickly switch the point of attack from the left to the right.

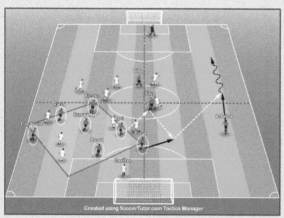

The situation created in this area is a 4 (+3) v 4 as shown in the diamond zone.

The ball is moved very well with short passes and good support/movement (pass, 1-2 combination etc) from one side to the other.

Arbeloa uses the full width of the pitch and Pique passes to him into the large space on the right in the opposition's middle zone.

Arbeloa dribbles forward very quickly and Silva, Xavi, Riera and Villa also show fast running to get forward and support him in and outside of the opposition's penalty area.

Arbeloa passes to Silva and he dribbles the ball inside.

The defenders do not close down Silva quick enough and with an excellent finish he scores in the far corner.

(If 1 or 2 defenders who were near to Villa and Riera had closed down Silva, he also had the solution to pass to his teammates in the penalty area).

SESSION FOR THIS TOPIC *(5 Practices)*

1. Possession Play & Pressing in a 7 v 4 Transition Game

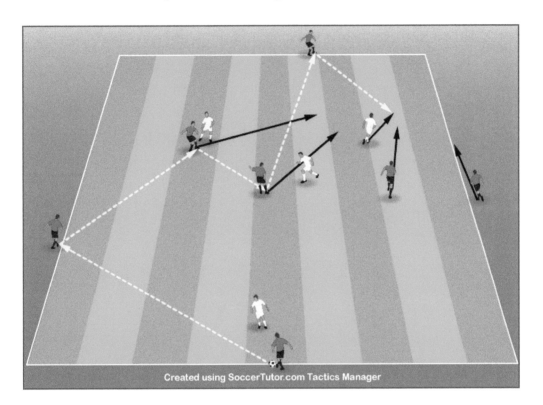

Created using SoccerTutor.com Tactics Manager

Objective

We work on keeping possession and immediate pressing when the ball is lost (to close the time and space).

Description

In an area 18 x 12 yards we work with 11 players. The red team have 7 players with 4 players on the sides of the grid and 3 players inside. The whites have 4 players all inside. At the bottom and at the top we use centre backs and attacking midfielders or strikers. At the sides we use full backs or wide midfielders/forwards. On the inside we use central midfield players (CM, LCM or RCM).

The objective for the red team is to keep possession and if they lose the ball they make a quick transition to defence and try to win the ball back immediately. (With the ball - OPEN, when we lose the ball - CLOSE).

If the reds complete 8-10 passes they get 1 point, if the reds keep possession for 30 seconds they get 2 points. If the whites win the ball and complete 4-5 passes (or keep possession for 6 seconds) they get 1 point.

Rule

The 4 outside red players are limited to 2 touches, the 3 inside red players have 1 touch and the white players have unlimited touches.

149

PROGRESSION
2. Possession Play & Pressing in a 4 (+3) v 4 Transition Game

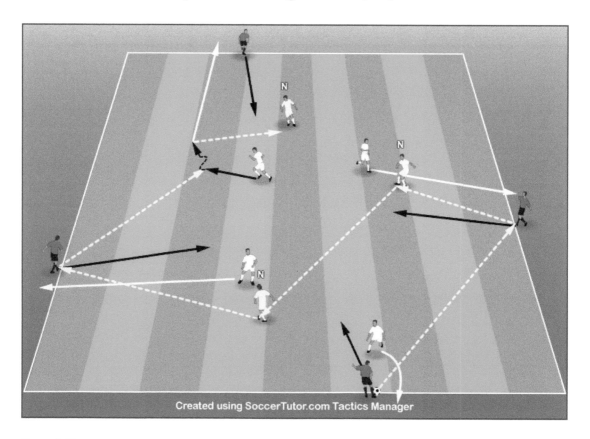

Created using SoccerTutor.com Tactics Manager

Description

In this progression to the previous drill we now have 2 teams of 4 and 3 neutral players (inside) who always play with the team in possession. The team which starts with the ball have all their players at the sides.

The objective for the reds is the same again but when the whites win the ball, both teams change roles and make a transition from attack to defence and defence to attack respectively (the whites take the positions at the sides and start possession as the reds move inside and start to press the ball).

Different Rules

1. All players have are limited to 2 touches.
2. All players are limited to 2 touches and the neutrals have 1 touch.
3. All players are limited to 1 touch.

Coaching Points

1. The angles and distances of the support players should be monitored.
2. The timing, weight and accuracy of the passes is key to maintain possession.
3. Players need quick reactions to make a quick transition to defence or attack.

150

PROGRESSION

3. Attacking from the Back & Quickly Providing Support in a 2 Zone Possession Game (2)

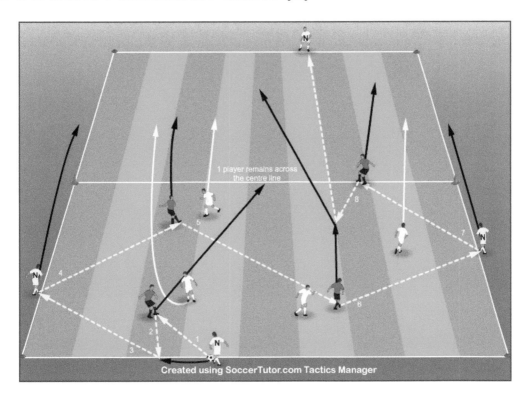

Created using SoccerTutor.com Tactics Manager

Description

We mark out 2 grids 18 x 12 yards each and work with 2 teams of 4 with 4 extra neutral players.

The practice starts with one team in the first grid and the players keep possession as shown in the diagram with the help of the 3 neutrals in the positions shown. 1 player from the team in possession can only move along the halfway line and all other players are positioned inside. The 4 defenders (white) are all inside and we have a 4 (+3) v 4 situation.

The objective for the team in possession is to complete 6-8 passes in one grid and then pass the ball to the other grid. If this happens all players (except the 1 neutral at the end) move across to the other grid and continue with the same objective. A new player moves to the halfway line position and we again have a 4 (+3) v 4.

If the team defending (white in diagram example) win the ball they have 2 options:

1. At first they must complete 6-8 passes in the same grid and after can change grid.
2. Progress to them passing immediately to the other grid and moving quickly across to start their possession (a white player must move to the halfway line position).

Rule

All players a are limited to 2 touches (or 1) / All players are limited to 2 touches and the neutrals have 1 touch.

PROGRESSION
4. Possession & Pressing in a Continuous 4 Grid Transition Game

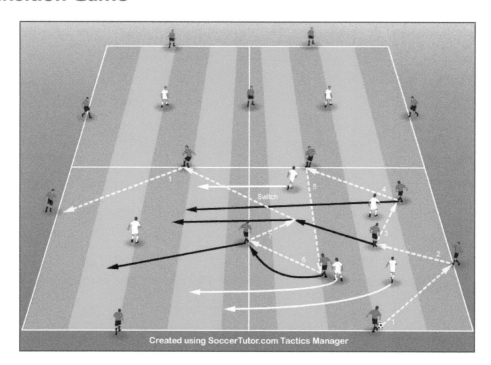

Created using SoccerTutor.com Tactics Manager

Objective
To develop short passes, maintaining possession in a 4 (+3) v 4 situation and switching the point of attack.

Description
We now mark out 4 grids (12 x 12 yards each). We work with 22 players with 15 red players and 7 white players. The players are in the positions shown in the diagram. We always have 3 red players inside one grid and 4 outside with 4 white players inside. 1 more white player is positioned in each of the other 3 grids.

The practice starts in one grid with a 4 (+3) v 4 situation. The objective is to complete 6-8 passes within the grid and then pass the ball into another grid where the numerical situation is the same.

2 inside red players and 3 white players move across to the next grid to again play inside. The outside player on the line between the 2 zones also moves across to play now play on the inside and his position is taken by the other red inside player. The practice continues with the aim of passing through all 4 grids.

If the whites win the ball they try to keep possession in the same grid and the 7 red players make a negative transition and must win the ball back within 6 seconds. If the whites keep possession for 6 seconds or complete 4-5 passes they get 1 point.

Different Rules
1. All red players are limited to 2 touches.
2. All red players are limited to 1 touch.

PROGRESSION
5. Keeping Possession in the Low Zone, Switching Play & Fast Attacks in an 11 v 11 Zonal Game

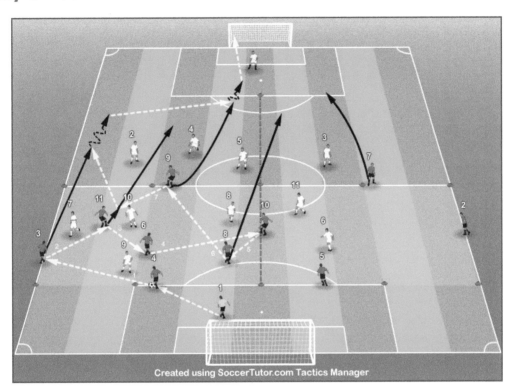

Created using SoccerTutor.com Tactics Manager

Description

Using a full pitch we split it down the middle with a line from one box to the other. We also create 2 grids in the area in between 1 box and the halfway line. We play an 11v11 game with the red team in a 4-4-2 formation (with a bowl) and the white team in a 4-2-3-1 or 4-4-2.

The game always starts with the reds in possession, building up from the back. The players are in the positions shown in the diagram. When playing in the left grid we have a 7v4 situation + 3 white defenders outside.

In the right grid we have a 3 (+1) v 2 (+1) situation with 1 red centre back (5), the right back (2) and the second striker (7). The objective for the red team is:

1. To keep possession in one grid and complete 6-8 passes there before changing the point of attack to the other grid and launching a fast attack from there.

2. To keep possession in one grid and complete 6-8 passes there before changing the point of attack to the other grid and creating a new 7v4 situation there, keeping possession again (6-8 passes) before changing the point of attack again back to the starting grid and launch the fast attack from there.

If the white team win the ball, they attack and try to score (counts double if they do). This rule means the reds are forced to move very quickly from attack to defence. All players move in quickly and close the space. If they win the ball back, they open up again and take their original positions and start the drill again.

CHAPTER 4

The Transition from Defence to Attack in the Low Zone

SPAIN Attacking Sessions

The Transition from Defence to Attack in the Low Zone

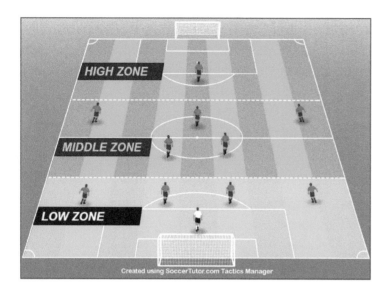

During this transition Spain scored a total of 8 goals (3 at Euro 2008, 2 goals in qualifying for the World Cup in South Africa and 3 goals at the finals in 2010).

After this tournament, Spain did not score any more goals from this phase of the game.

This is because the vast majority of teams playing against Spain in the last 3 years defended in the low zone and the middle zone and very rarely (or not at all) in the high zone.

Spain scored 1 goal with a fast break attack after an opponent's corner and quickly exploited the free space in behind the opposition's defensive line. In this situation, Spain used the great technical qualities of the players they had in all positions, such as Capdevila at the back, Iniesta in the middle and Villa in attack.

Spain scored 3 goals playing a very fast long first ball into the opposition half and taking advantage of the 1v1 or 2v2 situations (exploiting the speed, quality and creativity of their attackers).

Another solution was displayed against Bosnia when Spain had a transition from the low zone playing direct forward passes through the zones. They displayed a high quality of passes, individual technique (dribbling, feints) and creativity. The objective was to bypass the lines of the opposition and play the ball in behind. The final objective is to pass the ball in

behind the defensive line in between the full back and the centre back. This is an area where Spain had an advantage with their fast players, energy, speed of movement and also the speed of their decision making.

Against Honduras, Spain worked very well in a ball oriented defence with good positions, distances and shape between the lines and move into a transition in an open pitch with an equality of numbers (4v4) for the attack. The 4th goal against Russia was scored with a fast break attack and overload game situation.

Finally, the most important goal in the Spanish national team's history was made through a slow transition situation where the players had a numerical disadvantage. They maintained possession under pressure and they attacked the weakest point of the Netherlands defence (Iniesta goal in the World Cup final 2010).

GOAL ANALYSIS
Quick Transition to Attack when Defending a Corner Kick
10-Jun-2008: European Championship 2008 Qualifying

Spain 4-1 Russia (2nd Goal): Villa - Assist: Iniesta
Spain in a 4-1-3-2 vs Russia in a 4-1-4-1 (and from 70' in a 3-4-1-2)

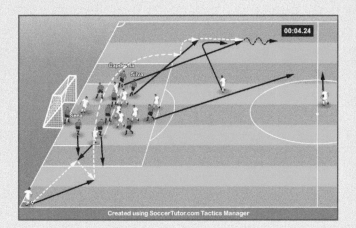

Russia had a corner on the left with 7 players in the box, 1 outside and 1 defender on the halfway line. Spain have all their players in the box; 1 near post, 2 in front of the GK (near and far post) and the others in a 4-2-1 formation.

The corner is taken short and the cross is not good. The ball goes to the other side of the pitch. The nearest player (Silva) runs quickly to the ball and Capdevila provides support with a diagonal cutting run in behind the opponent. Capdevila receives and dribbles forward with the ball.

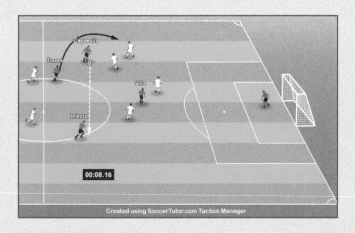

Capdevila crosses the halfway line and 3 other players run quickly forward to support him.

Villa goes central, Torres makes an overlapping run and Iniesta provides support inside for him.

Capdevila passes to Iniesta and Spain are attacking in a 4v4 (+2) situation.

SPAIN Attacking Sessions

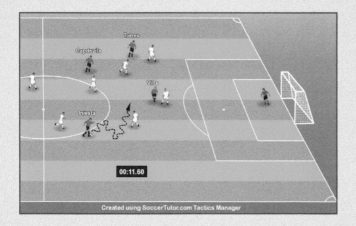

Iniesta dribbles the ball with good technical skills and feints, changes direction with the ball to create space to pass the ball to Villa.

Torres and Capdevila stay on the left and do not enter the box so that they leave the space to Villa who is faster.

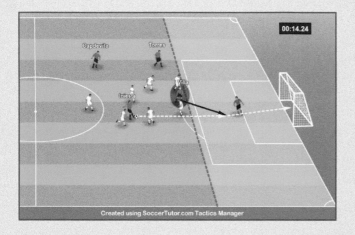

Villa makes a run in between the 2 central defenders and Iniesta passes to him in the space with the correct timing.

Villa shoots first time and scores.

From Silva's first touch to the goal it took 14.24 seconds.

SESSION FOR THIS TOPIC *(5 Practices)*

1. Quick Passing Combination, Diagonal Runs & Dribbling Practice

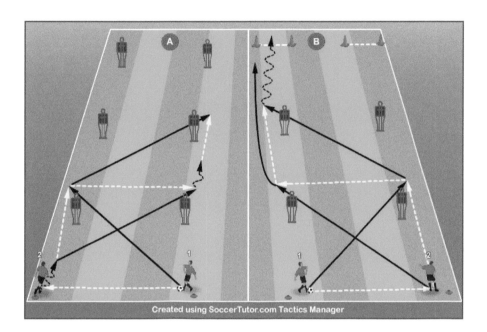

Created using SoccerTutor.com Tactics Manager

Objective

To develop the movement in behind the opposition with diagonal runs, combination play with a teammate and running with the ball at speed.

Description

A) In an area 18 x 8 yards, we work with 2 players and we have 2 cones and 6 mannequins. Player 1 passes to Player 2 and makes a fast diagonal cutting run in behind the left mannequin. Player 2 takes a directional first touch, passes to player 1 and moves diagonally in front of the other mannequin. Player 1 passes again to player 2 and now makes the same movement in the other direction as the sequence continues.

B) This is a progression and we now have 2 small cones, 4 large cones and 4 mannequins. The objective is the same as in part A, but after the second diagonal cutting run from player 1, he has a second objective to dribble the ball into the cone goal opposite (as shown). This should be done while being put under pressure from player 2 who runs across to stop it after playing their final pass.

Coaching Point

1. This practice should be done at high pace to replicate a fast break attack.
2. The passes need to be in front of the player and timed well to the movement (like passing in behind defence).
3. Good communication (verbal & optical) and awareness is needed to avoid collision and time passes/ movement.

159

PROGRESSION
2. Quick Passing Combination, 3rd Man Run & Dribbling Practice

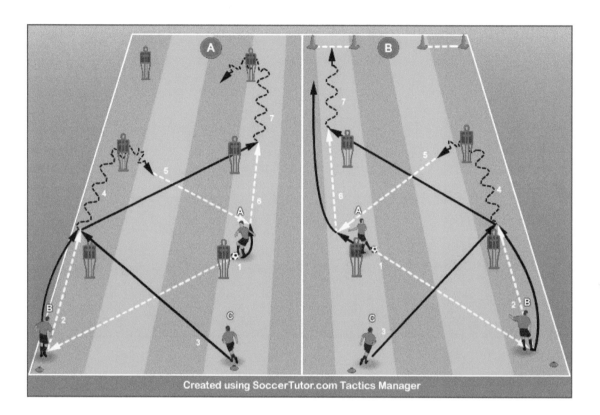

Created using SoccerTutor.com Tactics Manager

Description

In this progression we work with 3 players and we have 2 cones and 6 mannequins.

A) The drill starts with player A who passes diagonally to player B (as shown). At the same time, player 3 makes a fast diagonal run in front of the mannequin to the left and provides support in front of B who passes to him and moves forward himself.

Player C dribbles the ball around the next mannequin and passes to A. Now player B makes a fast diagonal cutting run in front of the mannequin to the right and A passes to him and moves forward, continuing the sequence.

B) We now have 2 small cones, 4 large cones and 4 mannequins. We have the same objective as in Part A, but after the second diagonal cutting run from player B, he has a second objective to dribble the ball into the cone goal opposite (as shown). This should be done while being put under pressure from A who runs across to stop it after playing the final pass.

All players pass from all positions and the drill is executed from both sides.

PROGRESSION
3. Fast Break Attack when Defending a Corner Kick: Exploiting the Opposite Flank

A

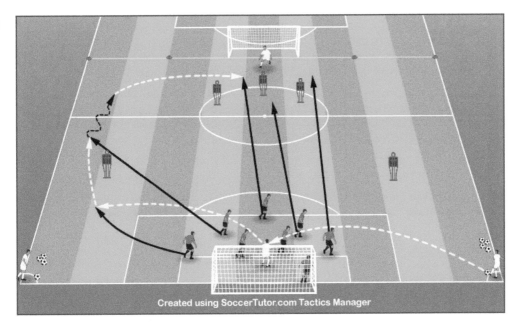

B

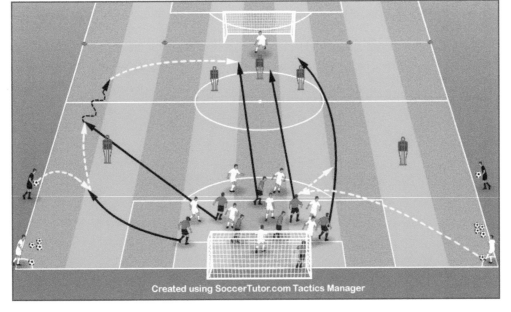

SPAIN Attacking Sessions

Objective

We work on defending a corner kick and launching a quick counter attack on the opposite flank.

Description

A) We use ¾ of a full pitch and position an extra goal as shown and we also put 5 mannequins in the positions presented in the diagram.

In the first stage we work with 9 players in the starting positions as displayed. On both sides we have coaches (or players) and many balls.

A coach or player from one side crosses the ball into the box and when the goalkeeper catches it, he rolls the ball out to a player moving on the opposite side to to where the corner was taken from.

A second player on this side makes a quick diagonal run in front of the mannequin and provides support. He receives the pass and dribbles past the halfway line and crosses the ball at the height of and round the back of the mannequins. At the same time, 3 other players have run from the box quickly to support; 1 to the near post, 1 to the far post and the other coming in behind them.

B) In this progression we now have fully active opponents for the corner kicks. If the red goalkeeper is able to catch the ball, the drill progresses like the first drill and the whites do not leave the penalty area.

If the red team head/clear the ball away, the coach on the other side plays another ball in from the flank (as we see in the diagram) and the red team are again in transition to attack with movements like before.

If the whites win the ball (shoot or score) another corner kick is taken and the process repeated.

Rules

1. From the time that the goalkeeper or coach pass the ball, the attack must finish in a maximum of 10 seconds.
2. All red players use 1-2 touches except the player who dribbles and crosses who has unlimited touches.
3. The player who makes the cutting run has 4-5 seconds before having to cross the ball.

Coaching Points

1. There should be a very quick movement by the first player to receive the ball from the coach and an explosive support movement from the second player to receive the pass in behind the mannequin.
2. Passing in behind the mannequin/s (defenders) needs to be well timed for the diagonal or forward run.
3. The passes need to be in front of players to run onto without breaking stride, which is very important for a successful fast break attack.
4. Free creativity and decision making is used to finish the attack.

PROGRESSION
4. Fast Break Attack when Defending a Corner Kick: Exploiting the Opposite Flank on a Full Pitch

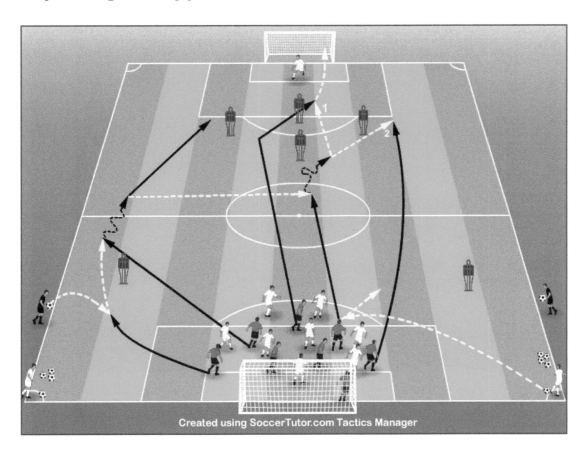

Created using SoccerTutor.com Tactics Manager

Objective
We work on defending a corner kick and launching a quick counter attack on the opposite flank.

Description
This is exactly the same as the previous drill, but now we are using a full sized pitch and have placed 4 mannequins (instead of 3) in the opposition half as shown in the diagram.

Rule
From the time that the goalkeeper or coach passes the ball, the attack must finish in a maximum of 12-14 seconds.

Coaching Point
The coaching points of the previous drill are still relevant, as the only thing that has changed is the size of the area used.

PROGRESSION

5. Fast Break Attack when Defending a Corner Kick: Exploiting the Opposite Flank in a Fully Active Game Situation

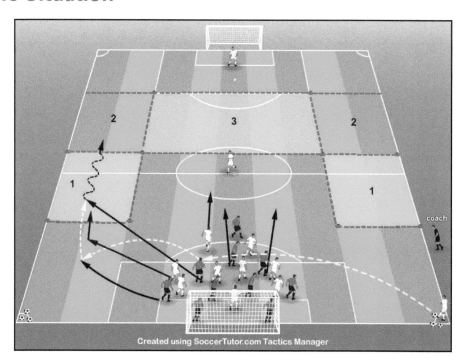

Created using SoccerTutor.com Tactics Manager

Description

Now in this progression we again use a full pitch and we create 5 areas as shown in the diagram. Areas 1 and 2 on both sides are 16 x 24 yards and area 3 is 32 x 30 yards. This time we play a normal game with both teams active (the whites track and defend the counter attack).

The drill starts from the white's corner kick and the objective for the red team is a) to defend the corner and b) make a quick transition from defence to attack. However, they must do this only from the 2 sides (area 1), receiving a pass inside this area and then dribbling into zone 2.

If this happens, the player who has the ball is not allowed beyond the zone 2 end line and has 2 options: **1.** Pass to zone 3 to a teammate or **2.** Pass from area 2 into the box to a teammate.

The defenders are not allowed to enter the final zone before the ball is played in there. When the ball goes out, we always start again with the opposition's corner kick (but change the side it is taken).

Rules

1. The red team players are limited to 1 or 2 touches in their half except for the player who moves into area 1.

2. In area 2, players have a maximum of 2-3 touches or 3-5 seconds to pass the ball into another area.

3. If the red team passes the ball to zone 2, they have a maximum of 6-10 seconds to complete the attack.

4. Only 1 white player from each team is allowed into zone 1 at a time.

GOAL ANALYSIS

Playing Quickly from Back to Front: Exploiting 1v1, 2v1 or 2v2 Situations in the Final Third (1)

10-Jun-2008: European Championship 2008 Qualifying

Spain 2-1 Sweden (2nd Goal): Villa - Assist: Capdevila

Spain in a 4-4-2 vs Sweden in a 4-4-2

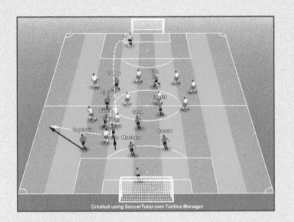

The Sweden goalkeeper plays the ball long and all players are positioned in the centre of the pitch.

Xavi loses the challenge in the air but the ball is headed on to Albiol who passes the ball to the side.

Capdevilla moves faster than his direct opponent to get to the ball first.

8 players from the Spanish team are in the defensive half of the pitch.

Capdevila plays a first time long pass up the line towards Torres.

Torres fights with his direct opponent, but the ball goes past both and into the box.

Villa is quickest to the ball and takes it under his possession.

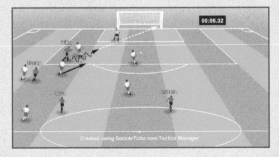

Villa is now in a 1v1 situation with the defender and displays good feints to dribble inside.

He is able to get the ball onto his right foot (strongest foot) and finishes strongly into the net.

The attack was completed in 6.32 seconds.

SPAIN Attacking Sessions

GOAL ANALYSIS

Playing Quickly from Back to Front: Exploiting 1v1, 2v1 or 2v2 Situations in the Final Third (2)

01-Apr-2009: World Cup 2010 Qualifying

Turkey 1-2 Spain (2nd Goal): Riera - Assist: Guiza

Spain in a 4-2-3-1 vs Turkey in a 4-4-2

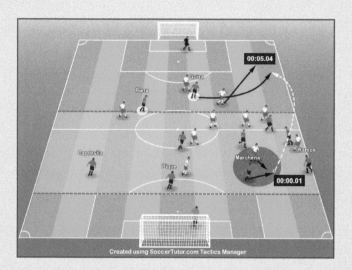

The same situation occurred against Turkey. There is an 8v8 in the marked out zone in the Spanish half of the pitch.

The ball goes into an area closest to Marchena and his opponent.

Marchena is quickest to the ball and with 1 touch makes a long pass up the right flank into the free space in the high zone of the pitch with the objective to find Guiza.

Guiza is running to the ball against one opponent in a 1v1 situation.

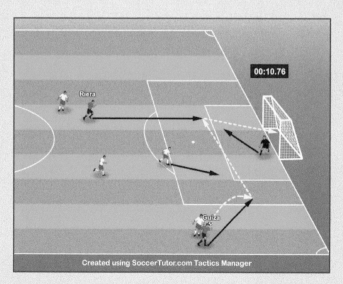

Guiza heads the ball into the space ahead and runs into the box, leaving the defender behind and winning the 1v1 battle.

Guiza is closed down by another defender and plays a good short cross across the penalty area to Riera, who has made a run from deep ahead of his direct opponent.

Riera scores with a first time shot.

This counter attack was completed in 10.76 seconds.

GOAL ANALYSIS

Playing Quickly from Back to Front: Exploiting 1v1, 2v1 or 2v2 Situations in the Final Third (3)

25-Jun-2010: World Cup 2010 Qualifying

Spain 2-1 Chile (1st Goal): Villa

Spain in a 4-3-2-1 vs Chile in a 4-3-3

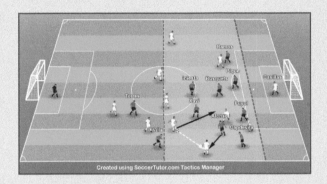

There are 8 players from both Chile and Spain in the zone shown within the Spanish half.

The Chile player passes to the right flank and makes a run inside.

Alonso presses the ball carrier who does not have good support from his teammates (no passing options).

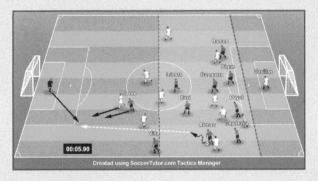

Alonso wins the ball and passes very quickly into the free space in the high zone on the left flank and in behind the last defender towards Torres who is now in a 1v1 situation with the defender.

Torres sprints to the ball against one defender and the goalkeeper, who leaves his penalty area to attempt to clear the ball.

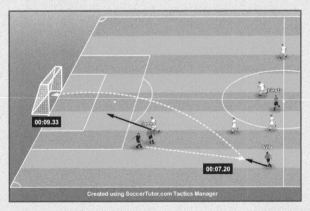

The goalkeeper, as he is put under pressure from Torres, makes a poor decision and clears the ball straight to David Villa.

Villa has an excellent first touch and produces a quality lob shot to score the goal.

This counter attack took 7.20 seconds.

SPAIN Attacking Sessions

SESSION FOR THIS TOPIC *(6 Practices)*

1. GROUP A: **Passing Exercise with 1v1 Duel**

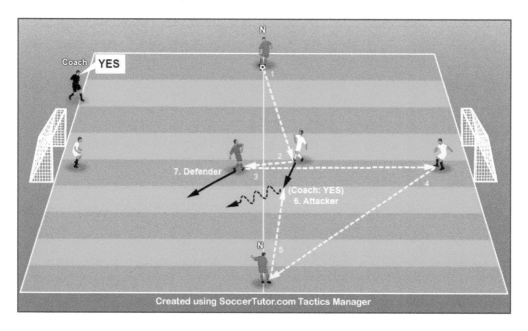

Objective

To develop quick reactions and dribbling/moves to beat in 1v1 situations.

Description

In an area 30 x 30 yards, we use 2 full sized goals with goalkeepers and 2 neutral players are positioned on the sidelines. Inside the playing area we have a 1v1 situation.

The drill starts with all 6 players passing the ball to each other freely, waiting for the coach's signal. When the coach gives the signal, the player inside who has the ball becomes the attacker and the other becomes the defender. If a goal is scored or the ball goes out, the drill starts from the beginning again.

Different Rules

1. When the defender wins the ball, the drill stops and starts from the beginning with another 2 players.
2. When the defender wins the ball, he becomes the attacker and the roles changes until the ball goes out of play.
3. The attackers have unlimited touches.
4. Limit the maximum amount of touches for the attacker.
5. The attackers have unlimited time to shoot.
6. The attackers have a limited time to shoot.

Coaching Point

The players need good concentration and quick reactions to respond to the coach's signal and then either attack or defend the goal immediately.

PROGRESSION
2. GROUP A: Possession and 1 v 1 Duels in a Dynamic 5 Zone Small Sided Game

Description

In an area 48 x 20 yards we create 5 zones. The 2 end zones are 10 x 20 yards, the middle zone is 18 x 20 yards and the 1v1 zones are both 5 x 20 yards.

In the middle zone we have a 4v4 situation and in the two 1v1 zones either side we have 1 defender from each team. On the sidelines we have 2 players from each team on each side (as shown). The practice starts with one team in possession (from the goalkeeper - red in diagram) and the defender in the 1v1 zone passes the ball to the middle zone.

The players in the middle zone keep possession and one player dribbles forward to play a 1v1 with the white defender in the next zone. If the red player wins the 1v1, he must use a maximum of 3 touches and shoot. The white defender then moves to the sideline and a teammate takes his place (as shown).

At the same time as the red player beats the defender, another white player from the side dribbles into the middle zone with a new ball. 1 red player also moves inside from the side (without a ball) and the practice continues with the whites now in possession.

If the defender wins the ball (in the 1v1 zone), he passes the ball back into the middle zone to a teammate. The attacker who lost the ball must also return to the middle zone again.

Rules
1. The defenders are not allowed in the end zones.
2. All players have unlimited touches, except in the final zone where they are limited to 3 touches.
3. Decide whether the team can pass back to the defender or not when trying to maintain possession.

PROGRESSION
3. GROUP A: 1v1 / 2v2 Duels in a 9 v 9 Small Sided Game

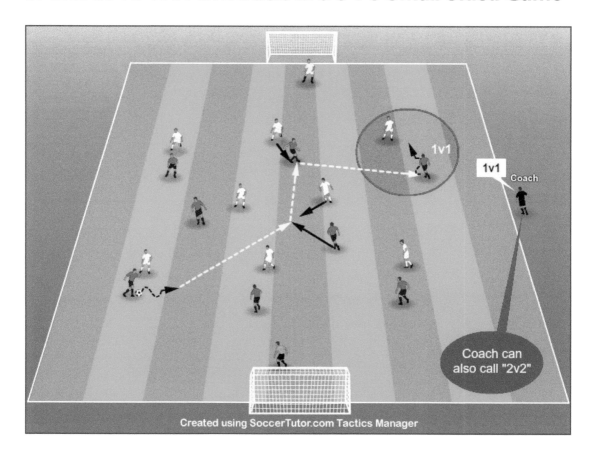

Created using SoccerTutor.com Tactics Manager

Objective
To develop quick reactions, dribbling, creativity and 1v1 / 2v2 attacking play within a small sided game.

Description
In an area 60 x 40 yards, we play 9v9. Both teams play a normal game with a 3-2-3 formation except:

1. When the coach gives the signal, the player who has the ball plays a 1v1 against his direct opponent (all other players from both teams are not allowed to participate).

2. When the coach gives the signal, the player who has the ball passes to a teammate and they both play a 2v2 against the 2 closest defenders (all other players from both teams are not allowed to participate).

3. We have 2 variables: If the coach says '1' we have a 1v1 situation and if he says '2' we have a 2v2 situation.

Different Rules
1. A completely free normal game.
2. Impose a limit to the time for the attackers to finish the 1v1 / 2v2 attack.
3. Unlimited time for the attackers to finish the 1v1 / 2v2 attack.

170

PROGRESSION
4. GROUP B: Press, Win the Ball & Quick Counter Attack with a Long Ball in a Position Specific Game

Objective
We work on defensive organisation, pressing to win the ball and launching a quick counter attack with accurate long passes.

Description
In the area shown in the diagram we have a goalkeeper and 8v8 outfield players. We mark out a line 3-5 yards past the halfway line. The red team is in a 4-4 formation and the white team are in a 2-4-2 (you can use any formation that you like).

The drill starts with the coach passing to the white team who try to score in the full sized goal. The objective for the red team is to use a ball orientated defence and win the ball. If they do, they must shoot immediately into one of the 2 small goals in the high zone.

As soon as a red player strikes the ball, the coach immediately passes a new ball in to a white player on the other side of the pitch. The reds must quickly switch their defensive organisation to the other side of the pitch.

Rules
1. From the moment the reds win the ball, they have 3-5 seconds to hit a long pass into one of the mini goals.
2. The red team are limited to 2-3 touches.
3. The white team have unlimited touches.
4. No player from either team can move beyond the the red line.

PROGRESSION

5. GROUP B: Press, Win the Ball & Quick Counter Attack with a Long Ball in a Position Specific Game (2)

A

B

Description

We still have the same zone marked out as before, but now we use the full pitch and have 2 goalkeepers and 2 boxes in the positions shown. In each box we put 1 red player (2 attackers from the 4-4-2).

A) We have the same objective as the previous practice, but now when the red team wins the ball they must play a quick long pass to 1 of the 2 attackers inside the boxes.

The attacker must control the ball within the box and when he dribbles out he passes the ball to a white player on the opposite side (as shown).

The red player who made the pass goes into the box and the player (attacker) switches positions with him after playing his pass. The white team must try to attack quickly and exploit the temporary numerical advantage and the imbalance of the red team. The red team must organise themselves very quickly and defend their goal.

B) 2 defenders and a goalkeeper are added to the practice. Now when the red team passes the ball from the low zone to the attackers, they must control the ball within the box and then dribble towards goal where they are faced with a 1v1 against a defender, who they must beat before trying to score past the goalkeeper.

While the ball is travelling to one of the attackers in the boxes, the coach immediately passes a new ball to the white team on the other side of the pitch. The reds must switch the point of their defensive organization to the other side of the pitch.

Rules

1. From the moment the red team wins the ball, they have 3-5 seconds to pass the ball to an attacker in a box.
2. The red attackers have a limited time to finish their attack (6-8 seconds).
3. The red team are limited to 2-3 touches.
4. The white team have unlimited touches.
5. No player from either team can move beyond the the red line.

Coaching Points

1. A quality first time ball is needed to achieve a quick transition from defence to attack with one long pass under pressure of time and space.
2. Players need to communicate and press together to win the ball from the opposition.
3. In Part B players should demonstrate creativity and technical skills to beat the defender, as well as quality finishing.

PROGRESSION

6. GROUP A & B: Press, Win the Ball & Quick Counter Attack with a Long Ball - 2 v 2 Support Play in a 3 Zone Game

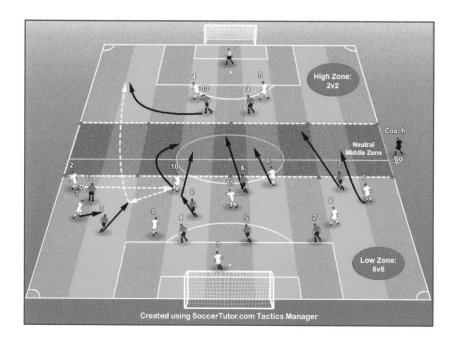

Objective

We work on defensive organisation, pressing to win the ball and launching quick counter attacks with accurate long passes.

Description

The final game for this session is on a full sized pitch. We mark out a neutral zone (20 x 65 yards) 5 yards into one half of the pitch and 15 yards into the other, as shown.

In the low zone we have an 8v8 situation with the red team playing 4-4 and the white team have 2 full backs, 4 midfielders & 2 attackers. In the high zone we have a 2v2 situation between 2 attackers and 2 centre backs. The attackers starting position is central and they ask for the ball on the flanks.

The drill starts with the white team in possession and they try to score. The red team play with a ball oriented defence and if they win the ball in the low zone, they must pass quickly to the 2 attackers in the high zone.

In the beginning the 2 attackers play a 2v2 without any extra players allowed into this zone. After, progress so that when the ball goes from the low to the high zone, all players can move freely to support.

Rules

1. If the red team win the ball, they have 3-5 seconds to pass the ball to the attackers in the high zone.
2. The red team are limited to 2-3 touches in the low zone.
3. The 2 attackers from the red team have unlimited touches.
4. The white team have unlimited touches.
5. From the moment the red defenders win the ball, the attack must finish within 6-12 seconds.
6. From the moment a red attacker receives the ball, the attack must finish within 6-8 seconds.

GOAL ANALYSIS

Transition to Attack from the Low Zone: Passing through the Lines

06-Sep-2008: World Cup 2010 Qualifying

Spain 1-0 Bosnia Hz (1st Goal): Villa - Assist: Xavi

Spain in 4-1-4-1 vs Bosnia Hz in a 3-5-2

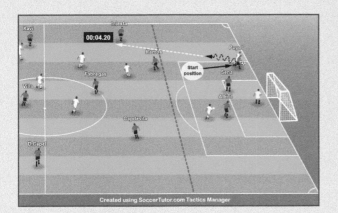

In the low zone we have a 3v2 situation.

Puyol wins the 1v1 with the attacker and takes the ball from him near the byline.

Puyol dribbles forward with the ball and passes to Iniesta who is on the right side of the middle zone.

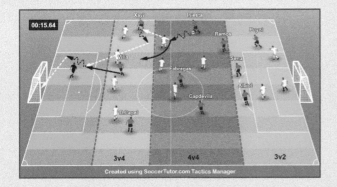

In the middle zone we have a 4v4 situation.

Iniesta dribbles the ball up to the high zone and when he is closed down, he passes to Xavi on his right. Xavi dribbles inside and when he has the opportunity to pass to Villa, he makes an excellent pass into the space behind the back 4 (between the left back and the centre back).

Villa moves at the right time, dribbling round the goalkeeper and scores.

In the 3rd zone before the ball goes into the 4th zone, we have a 3 (+1) vs 4.

From the time that Puyol won the ball deep in his own half to Villa scoring, it took 15.54 seconds.

SPAIN Attacking Sessions

SESSION FOR THIS TOPIC *(4 Practices)*

1. Building Up Play Quickly Through the Lines Small Sided Games

A

B

SPAIN Attacking Sessions

Objective

We work on building up play from back to front quickly through the lines of the opposition.

Description

A) In an area 32 x 16 yards we mark out 3 zones. The 2 end zones are 9 x 16 yards and the central zone is 14 x 16 yards. In the 2 end zones we have a 2v2 (+1 neutral player) and in the centre zone we have a 3v3 (+1 neutral player) situation. The neutral players always play with the team who has possession.

The drill starts with the goalkeeper who passes to a defender. The objective is to pass the ball very quickly to the central zone and the objective in the central zone is to pass quickly to the final zone.

Finally in the end zone, the objective is to quickly pass the ball to the other goalkeeper (not to score). The goalkeeper then passes the ball to one of his teammates (white) and they now have the same objective going in the opposite direction.

B) In this progression we remove the 2 neutral players from the end zones and instead have 3v2 situations. Now one player from the middle zone must dribble into the end zone to create a 3v3 situation and this time the attackers try to score in the goal.

Rules (Part A)

1. Each player is only allowed to make 2 passes.
2. The neutral players are limited to 1 touch.
3. The ball must move from one goalkeeper to the other within a set amount of time (e.g. 8-10 seconds).

Variations

1. The defenders play passive defence / The defenders play active defence.
2. High press to the ball but they are not allowed to tackle their opponents.
3. The defenders can only press to try and block passes.
4. The defenders are fully active and can tackle their opponents.

Rules (Part B)

The same as above except that all players have a maximum of 2 passes in the low zone, 3 touches in the middle zone and have unlimited touches in the final zone.

Coaching Points

1. Players should check away from their markers before moving to receive (create space).
2. The players should mainly use direct passes to feet when playing through the lines.
3. Encourage players to dribble with the ball and change direction at speed.
4. In Part B good communication, decision making and finishing is needed in the final third.

PROGRESSION

2. Quick Transition to Attack from the Back in a 3 Zone Small Sided Game

Created using SoccerTutor.com Tactics Manager

Objective

We work on building up play from back to front quickly through the lines of the opposition. This time we have the help of 3 neutral players (2 of which provide width).

Description

In this progression we add 2 extra neutral players on the sides (as shown). These players can move and support only in the middle and the high zones, playing with the team who have possession of the ball.

Rule

The attack must finish in a maximum of 10 seconds.

Coaching Points

1. The final pass needs to be with the correct weight and well timed to the movement in behind the defensive line.
2. The coaching points from the previous small sided games are relevant again here.

PROGRESSION
3. Winning the Ball & Quick Transition to Attack in a Dynamic 4 Zone Game

Created using SoccerTutor.com Tactics Manager

Objective
We work on building up play from back to front quickly through the lines of the opposition on a full pitch.

Description
Now we use a full pitch and create 4 zones as shown in the diagram. We have a 3v2, a 4v4 (+1 neutral player) and 2v3 situations in the first 3 grids. We also have 2 neutral players positioned at the side who can only move between zones 2 and 3.

To score a goal, the team in possession must follow certain rules when moving through the zones. If a defender wins the ball in zone 1, they must pass quickly pass to zone 2. From zone 2, a player must dribble the ball into zone 3. Finally from zone 3 to 4, a player must pass into the space behind the defensive line for a teammate.

When one team finishes their attack (or the ball goes out of play) the team roles change. The ball starts with the other goalkeeper. In the diagram, once the reds have finished their attack, the white goalkeeper would start with the ball and the numerical situations in the first 3 zones are shown on the left side (3v2 in zone 1).

Rules
1. In zones 1 and 4 the players are limited to 2 touches. In zones 2 and 3 they have unlimited touches.
2. When a team wins the ball in zone 1, they have a maximum of 15 second to finish their attack.
3. When a team wins the ball in zone 2, they have a maximum of 10 second to finish their attack.

PROGRESSION
4. Winning the Ball & Quick Transition to Attack in an 11 v 11 Dynamic 4 Zone Game

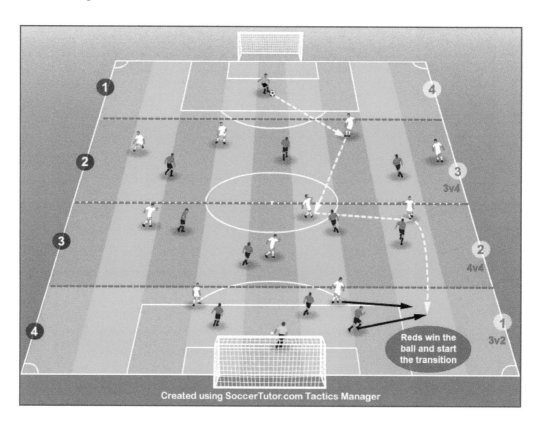

Created using SoccerTutor.com Tactics Manager

Description

Here we use the same 4 zones, but all the neutral players have been removed. We have an 11v11 game situation.

When one team is in possession, the other team (in diagram the red team) start their defence in zone 3 with a 3v4 situation. In zone 2 we have a 4v4 situation and finally in zone 1 we have a 3v2 situation. The team in possession uses a 4-4-2 formation and the defending team are in a 3-4-3 formation.

The team building up from the back has an initial 4v3 advantage (zone 3). The best opportunity for the defending team to win the ball is in zones 2 and 1. When this happens they quickly move into transition to attack. This time their are no restrictions and the red team can counter attack with freedom of decision making.

Rules

1. In zone 1 the players are limited to 2 touches, zone 2 is 3 touches and in zones 3 & 4 they have unlimited touches.

2. In zones 1 & 4 the players are limited to 2 touches, zone 2 unlimited touches, and zone 3 is 3 touches.

3. If a team wins the ball in zone 1, they have a maximum of 15 seconds to finish their attack.

180

GOAL ANALYSIS

Transition to Attack from the Low Zone: (4 v 3 +1 Situation)

21-Jun-10: World Cup 2010 Group Match

Spain 2-0 Honduras (2nd Goal): Villa - Assist: J. Navas

Spain in a 4-3-3 vs Honduras in a 4-4-1-1

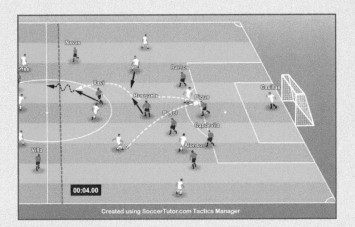

In the Spanish half we have 8 outfield players from Spain and 7 from the opposition.

The Honduras player tried to play a lofted ball in behind the defensive line, but the Spanish team has good defensive organisation and shape.

Pique is in a good position and heads the ball away.

The ball goes between Busquets and his direct opponent. Busquets gets there first and passes the ball in front of Xavi who runs forward onto the ball.

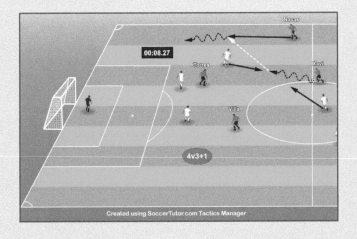

Xavi dribbles the ball forwards and Spain have made a transition from defence to attack and now have a 4v3 (+1) situation.

The left back closes down Xavi which creates free space on the right flank for Navas. Xavi recognises the situation well and passes at the correct time to Navas who has run up the right flank to support him.

Navas receives and dribbles the ball forward.

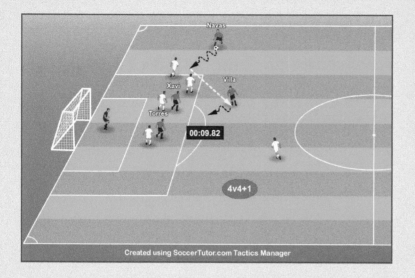

Navas now dribbles the ball inside and when the opponent closes the space in the penalty area, he passes inside to Villa who has come from the left to support him.

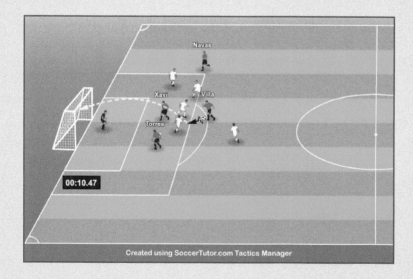

Villa takes a good directional first touch to the left which gives him the opportunity to shoot with his second touch.

The shot takes a deflection off of a defender and goes into the net.

The attack took 10.47 seconds.

SESSION FOR THIS TOPIC *(4 Practices)*

1. GROUP A: Win the Ball, Counter Attack & Quick Negative Transition (Switching the Point of Defence)

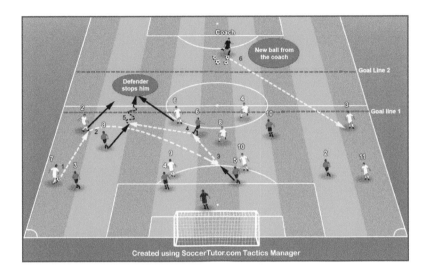

Objective

We work on winning the ball with a numerical disadvantage (7v9) and switching the point of defence in a quick negative transition.

Description

We have one goal line 5 yards inside the halfway line and another 75 yards from goal. In half a pitch we have 1 goalkeeper and 7 outfield players for the red team in a 4-3 formation and 9 players for the white team who are in a 4-2-3-1 formation (without 1 centre back).

The drill starts with the coach passing to a white player and the white team try to score. The red team play a ball oriented defence with a 7v9 numerical disadvantage. If they win the ball (reds) they have 2 objectives:

1. If they pass the first goal line they score 1 point (the white defenders can follow to stop them).

2. If they pass the final goal line they score 2 points.

3. When this happens, the coach immediately passes a new ball in the other direction, so the red team has a new objective to make a transition from attack to defence. They must switch the point of defence with a numerical disadvantage and work on basic principles of defensive organisation.

Rules

1. The white players have unlimited touches.

2. When the red team wins the ball, they have a limited time to pass the goal lines (6 seconds for the 1st goal line and 10 seconds for the 2nd goal line).

3. If the red team do not pass the goal lines in the set time, the coach can pass a new ball in for the white team.

Coaching Points

1. The defensive shape is key for the red team initially, keeping compact and in straight lines.

2. Explosive acceleration is needed to dribble past the defenders and through the goal lines.

3. The red team need quick reactions and organisation to switch their defence to the other side of the pitch.

SPAIN Attacking Sessions

2. GROUP B: Transition from Defence to Attack in a 4 v 5 (+2) Dynamic Zonal Game

The White team's objective is to keep possession; 8-10 consecutive passes = 1 Goal

Red player wins the ball and must make quick transition into attack and score any of the 2 goals

Objective

We work on winning the ball with a numerical disadvantage and fast break attacks.

Description

In an area 56 x 36 yards we divide the pitch into 3 zones. The central zone is 32 x 36 yards and the 2 end zones are 12 x 36 yards each. In the central zone we have 5 white players (2 at each end on the line as shown and 1 inside). We have 2 outside players who only play with the white team in possession. There are 4 red players inside.

The white team starts with possession of the ball and try to complete 8-10 passes (1 point). The red team aim to win the ball and make a fast transition to attack with the objective to score in either of the 2 goals.

When the red team attacks, the 2 white players on the line nearest the goal, the 1 inside player and 1 of the 2 players on the other line move to defend. This creates a 4 v 2 (+1 +1) or 4 v 3 (+1) situation.

Rules

1. The white players are limited to 2-3 touches and the blues have 1 touch.
2. The red players have unlimited touches in the central zone and 2 touches in the final zone.
3. When the red team win the ball they have a limited time to finish their attack (6-10 seconds).
4. Once the red team leave the central zone they have a limited time to finish their attack (4 seconds).

3. GROUP B: 6 v 6 Quick Reactions in a 2 Zone Transition Phase Game

PART 1

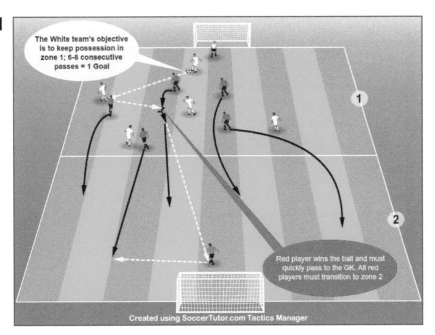

PART 2

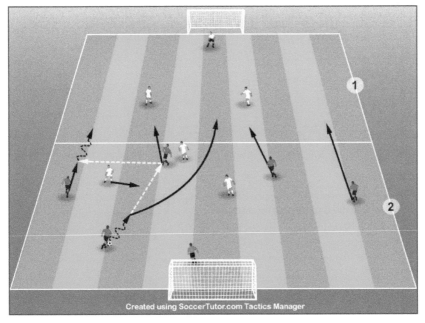

SPAIN Attacking Sessions

Objective

We work on keeping possession, winning the ball, fast break attacks and quick reactions in the transition phase.

Description

In an area 56 x 36 yards we divide the pitch into two 23 x 36 yard zones and play a 6v6 game. The team in possession use a free formation and the team who are defending press in a 2-3 formation.

Part 1

The drill starts in one grid and the white team has possession aiming to complete 6-8 passes to win 1 point. The first aim for the red team is to use collective pressing and win the ball.

If this happens, the second objective for the reds is to pass the ball to their goalkeeper. The goalkeeper passes to one of the red players and all 5 red players start a quick attack towards the other goal. At this moment, all players from both teams try to run across to the other zone (as shown).

Part 2 (Includes 2 Different Scenarios)

Scenario 1: Only the white players who manage to run into this half by the time all 5 red players have moved back can press and defend vs red team. The other players must stay in the other half and are out of the game for the moment.

In the example (2nd diagram) the red team moves into a fast attack vs 3 white players. The 3 white players can now defend across both zones (all the pitch) and they can return to the other grid once the ball is played in there.

Scenario 2: Only the white players who manage to run into this half by the time all 5 red players have moved back can press and try to defend vs red team. The other players must stay in the other half.

In the example (2nd diagram) the red team moves into a fast attack vs 3 white players in zone 2 (5v3). At first the 5 red players attack against the 3 white players in grid 2 and try to move the ball into the first grid. The 5 red players then attack against the 2 white players in grid 1 and try to score.

If a goal is scored or the ball goes out of play, the drill starts from the other side and the teams switch roles.

Rules

1. The team which starts in possession have unlimited touches.
2. When the defending team win the ball, they are limited to 2 touches until they pass to the goalkeeper.
3. Once the goalkeeper passes the ball, the reds have to finish their attack within a set time (e.g. 10 seconds).
4. If the reds score a goal they get 3 points.
5. In part 2, the white players in the second grid are not allowed to move back to the first grid and defend.

Coaching Points

1. The key elements of this transition game are the quick reactions and the awareness needed to be successful with a constantly changing game situation.
2. The attack shown in the Part 2 diagram needs to be done at pace with forward passes so that they are able to exploit the other team's lack of defensive shape before they reorganise.

PROGRESSION
4. Group A & B: Winning the Ball & 4 v 3 (+1) Fast Break Attacks in a 3 Zone Transition Game on a Full Pitch

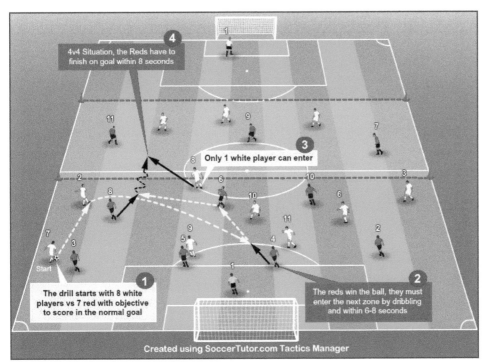

Objective

We work on keeping possession, winning the ball and fast break attacks 4v3 (+1) situation.

4v4 Situation, the Reds have to finish on goal within 8 seconds

Only 1 white player can enter

The drill starts with 8 white players vs 7 red with objective to score in the normal goal

The reds win the ball, they must enter the next zone by dribbling and within 6-8 seconds

Start

Created using SoccerTutor.com Tactics Manager

Description

We use a full pitch now and the area is split into 3 zones. There is a low zone with 1 red goalkeeper and 7 outfield players in a 4-3 formation and 8 white players in a 2-2-3-1 formation (2 full backs +2-3-1). In the other zone we have 3 red attackers and 3 white defenders and finally we have the white goalkeeper in the high zone.

The drill starts with an 8v7 and the white team are in possession with the objective to score in the goal. The red team's objective is to use good ball oriented defence and win the ball from the whites. 1 red player is then able to dribble into the next zone (followed by only 1 white player).

The red team must find solutions to finish the attack in a 4v3 (+1) attacking situation within a maximum of 8 seconds. All players are free to move into the final zone to attack/defend (whites - before ball is played in there).

Coaching Points

1. We work on good cooperation using quick combination play with the same tactical movements (allowing also for creativity) worked on previously in this session.
2. The red team need good defensive shape and collective pressing to win the ball in the low zone.
3. Fast and quality dribbling with the ball is required for the fast break attack in a 4v3 (+1) situation.
4. Quick finishing and decision making is also required under pressure of time and space in the final third.

GOAL ANALYSIS

Fast Break Attack

10-Jun-2008: European Championship 2008 Qualifying

Spain 4-1 Russia (4th Goal): Fabregas - Assist: Xavi

Spain in a 4-1-3-2

Russia are losing 3-1 and a lot of their players are high up the pitch. All of Russia's outfield players are in the Spanish half.

The Russian defender tries to pass back to his centre back. Villa reads the pass which is not hit with enough power.

Villa wins the ball and Spain make a transition to attack from the halfway line into the empty opposition half.

Villa dribbles forwards and is faced with a 1v1 situation.

Also, 2 opponents and Fabregas with Xavi are arriving fast from behind.

We have a 1v1 (+2v2) situation.

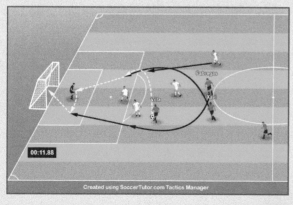

Fabregas and Xavi make opposite overlapping runs to support Villa.

Villa makes a lofted pass to Xavi who hits a first time volley. The goalkeeper saves and parries the ball to the left.

Fabregas was moving forward and shows good finishing with his head to score.

This counter attack took 11.88 seconds.

SESSION FOR THIS TOPIC *(4 Practices)*

1. Fast Break Attack with Support Play 1 v 1 (+2v2) Duel

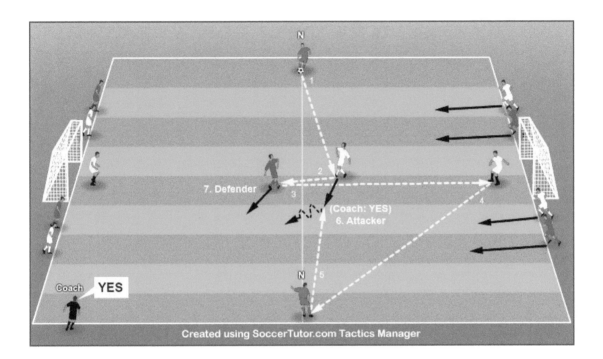

Created using SoccerTutor.com Tactics Manager

Objective

We practice fast break attacks with support players to practice the 1v1 (+2v2) situation.

Description

In an area 40 x 20 yards we have 2 full sized goals with 2 goalkeepers and 2 pairs of players at each end to the sides of the goals. At the sides we have 2 neutral players (red) and inside there are 2 players (1v1 situation).

The drill starts with a neutral player and all the players (2 inside, 2 neutrals & 2 goalkeepers) pass the ball around to each other waiting for the coaches signal.

When the coach gives the signal, the player who has the ball becomes the attacker and the other becomes the defender. The 2 pairs on the attackers side join the game to attack/defend. We have a 1v1 (+2v2) situation with the whites attacking and the blues defending.

If a goal is scored or the ball goes out of play, start the drill again with a different pair starting inside.

Coaching Points

1. The players on the side need to be fully concentrated so they can offer quick support.
2. Encourage creativity for the different attacking combinations.

VARIATION
2. Fast Break Attack with Support Play 1 v 1 (+2v2) Duel (2)

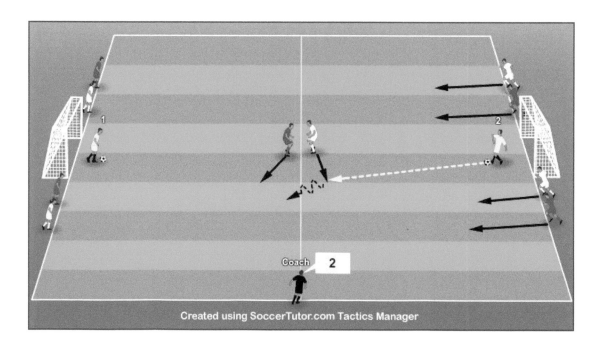

Created using SoccerTutor.com Tactics Manager

Description

This variation is the same as the previous practice, except the neutral players are removed and the goalkeepers are given a number (1 and 2). Both goalkeepers start with a ball.

The 2 inside players start face to face and must be ready for a quick reaction. When the coach gives the signal (calling out '1' or '2') that goalkeeper passes the ball to his teammate and the drill continues just like before.

PROGRESSION
3. Dynamic 3 v 3 Quick Transition Game

Created using SoccerTutor.com Tactics Manager

Objective

We work on quick reactions and fast transitions to finish attacks.

Description

In an area 40 x 20 yards, we have 2 goalkeepers and a 3v3 situation inside. There are also 2 pairs of players at each end to the sides of the goals.

The drill starts with a free 3v3 game inside and when the attack is finished, the coach passes a new ball to a player on the other team. That player and his direct opponent stay inside and the other 2 pairs leave the area.

Immediately the 2 pairs from the nearest end move inside and we have a continuous 1v1 (+2v2) game situation.

Coaching Points

1. Encourage attacking combinations between 2-3 players such as overlapping runs.
2. The focus here is to train the players to attack/defend in a 1v1 (+2v2) situation.
3. Players need to show good dribbling skills and changes of direction to create space.
4. Good communication, decision making and finishing is required in the attacking combinations (to finish attack quickly).

SPAIN Attacking Sessions

VARIATION
4. Dynamic 3 v 3 Quick Transition Game (2)

Created using SoccerTutor.com Tactics Manager

Description

We have 2 teams of 3 outfield players again here, but the outside players have been replaced with 4 poles as shown. Each player is assigned a number (1-3).

The drill starts with a 3v3 game and if a goal is scored or the ball goes out of play, the coach calls out a number (from 1 to 3).

The pairs who have the number that is called out stay inside and the coach passes to one of them.

The other 2 pairs must run quickly around one of the poles and then rejoin the game. This means we have a continuous 1v1 (+2v2) game situation.

Coaching Point

This drill should have a very high intensity and we must take care with the duration of the exercise, the size of the area, the number of the repetitions and the time in between repetitions etc (all depends on the age/ level of the players).

GOAL ANALYSIS

Transition to Attack with a Numerical Disadvantage in the Opposition Half

10-Jun-2010: World Cup 2010 Final

Spain 1-0 Netherlands: Iniesta - Assist: Xavi

Spain in a 4-2-3-1 vs the Netherlands in a 4-2-3-1

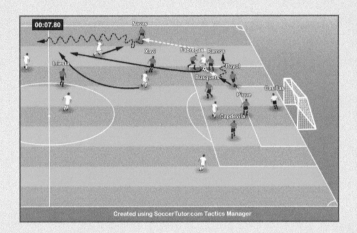

The Netherlands have 6 players and Spain have 9 players the Spanish half.

The Netherlands left forward is put under pressure from Ramos and Fabregas with Puyol providing defensive cover.

Puyol wins possession and dribbles the ball outside of the box to the right and passes to Navas.

Navas receives, dribbles past the opponent and enters the other half.

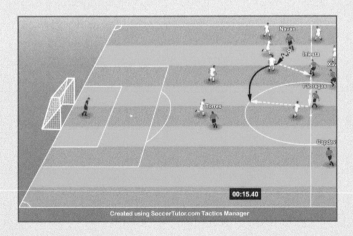

Navas is fresh off the bench and has the stamina to keep dribbling, goes up to the next opponent, passes inside to Iniesta and keeps running to provide good support.

Iniesta passes to Fabregas and Fabregas passes to Navas again who has moved inside.

Navas passes left to Torres and the Netherlands players make a very quick transition to defence.

The highlighted area shows that we have a 4 v 7 situation.

Spain try to keep possession and attack with a numerical disadvantage.

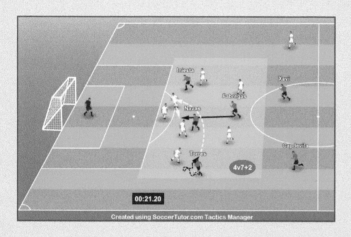

Torres touches the ball inside onto his right foot and tries to find Iniesta who is running into the space behind the defensive line.

Fabregas, at the same time, makes a straight run towards the penalty area.

The pass is blocked by the defender but the ball rebounds into the space which Fabregas is moving into.

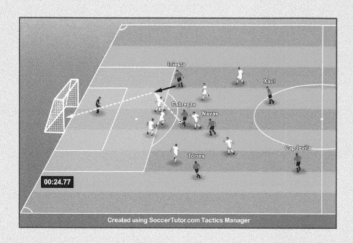

The Netherlands left back had moved inside and now the Netherlands defensive line is imbalanced on the left side.

Fabregas immediately recognises the situation and passes to Iniesta on the right side of the box.

Iniesta displays first class finishing by scoring the goal and wins the Spanish National team the World Cup.

SESSION FOR THIS TOPIC *(3 Practices)*

1. Possession Play with a Numerical Disadvantage in a 2 Zone Dynamic Transition Game

PART 1

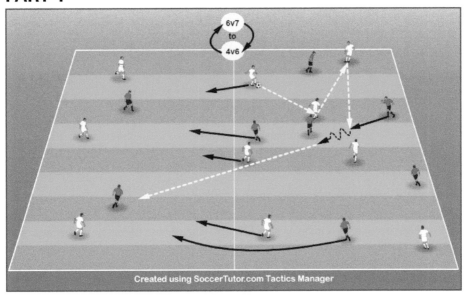

PART 2

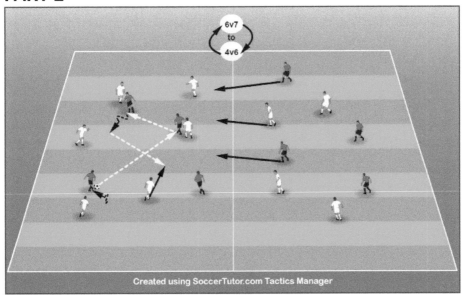

SPAIN Attacking Sessions

Objective

We work on our passing and movement to maintain possession and quick transition play with a numerical disadvantage.

Description

In an area 50 x 45 yards, we divide the pitch into 2 zones of 25 x 45 yards. We have 2 teams, one with 10 players and the other with 8 players.

The drill starts in one grid with a 6v7 situation. The objective for the 6 players is to win the ball and pass to their 2 teammates in the other grid.

Once they do, 2 players from the red team move across along with 3 players from the white team. Now we have the red team with a numerical disadvantage again (4v6) but this time they are in possession.

The red team must try to keep the ball as long as they can. If they lose possession, 1 white player and 2 red players move across from the other side and we have the same 6v7 situation again.

Rules

1. The white team are limited to 2-3 touches and the red team have unlimited touches.
2. If the white team complete 6-8 passes they get 1 point.
3. If the red team complete 4-6 passes they get 1 point.
4. If the red team keep the ball for 10 seconds they get 2 points.

Coaching Points

1. When trying to win the ball in a numerical disadvantage, players need to press together and reduce the time and space available to the opponent/s.
2. The key to the second part is being precise (and cautious) to maintain possession with a numerical disadvantage. Players need to protect (shield) the ball, using their body as a barrier between the opponent and the ball.
3. Players should check away from their marker before moving to receive.
4. Quick support movement is even more important with a numerical disadvantage.

SPAIN Attacking Sessions

PROGRESSION

2. Possession Play with a Numerical Disadvantage in a 3 Zone Dynamic Transition Game

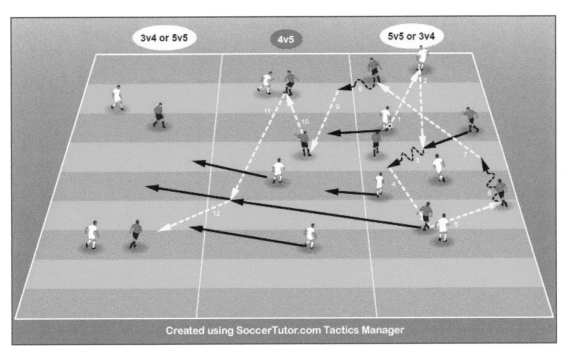

Description

In an area 60 x 30 yards we divide the pitch into 3 equal zones (20 x 30 yards). We have 10 white players and 9 red. In the first zone we have 5v5, in the second we have 2v3 and in the third zone we have a 2v2 situation.

The drills starts in zone 1 with the white team in possession and they aim to complete 6-8 passes (1 point). The red team press them and if they win the ball, the objective it is to then pass the ball to their 2 teammates in the middle zone. 2 red and 2 white players move across to create a 4v5 situation.

The aim for the red team in the middle zone is to complete 4-6 passes or keep the ball for 6-8 seconds. If the reds achieve this, they then pass the ball to the third grid to their 2 teammates. 1 red and 2 white players from the centre move across to create a 3v4 situation.

The aim for the reds in the third zone is to keep the ball for 6-8 seconds and then pass the ball back again to the middle zone (the drill is continuous). If the reds lose possession in the outside zone, we create 5v5 in there, 4v5 in the middle zone and 2v2 in the other side zone.

Rules

1. The white team are limited to 2-3 touches.
2. The red team have unlimited touches.
3. If the white team complete 6 passes they get 1 point / If the red team complete 4-6 passes they get 1 point.
4. If the red team keep the ball for 10 seconds they win 2 points.

PROGRESSION
3. Possession Play with a Numerical Disadvantage in a 3 Zone Dynamic Transition Game on a Full Pitch

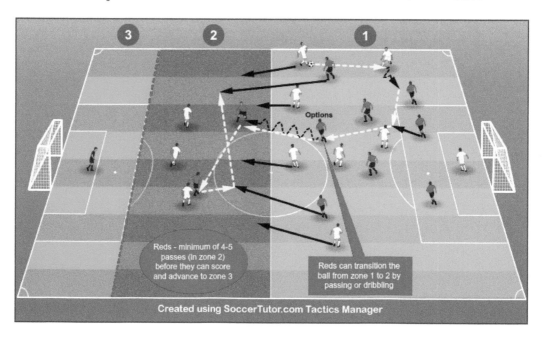

Reds - minimum of 4-5 passes (in zone 2) before they can score and advance to zone 3

Reds can transition the ball from zone 1 to 2 by passing or dribbling

Created using SoccerTutor.com Tactics Manager

Description

We use a full pitch now and create 3 zones again. The 3 numbered zones (1-3) are marked out as shown. The red team have 9 players in zone 1 and 2 players in zone 2. The white team have 7 players in zone 1 and 3 defenders in zone 2.

The drill starts with the white team in possession (zone 1) and they work to find solutions to score in the red's goal. The objective for the red team is to win the ball in zone 1 and then pass (or dribble) the ball into zone 2, where 2 red players and 4 white players can move across (from zone 1 to 2).

The red team are not allowed to attack the goal until they complete 4-5 passes or keep possession in zone 2 for 10 seconds. They must do this with a 4 v 7 disadvantage and then can enter the final zone (3) and shoot.

Rules

1. The red players in zone 1 have unlimited touches but they must pass to the next zone within 6-8 seconds from the moment they win the ball.
2. The red players have unlimited touches in zone 2 and are limited to 2 touches in zone 3 (final zone).
3. The white team have unlimited touches in all zones.

Coaching Points

1. The first step is to use good ball oriented defence in the low zone (collective pressing).
2. The focus here is keeping possession under pressure of a numerical disadvantage in the opposition half.
3. When they are able to attack in zone 2, the team should attack the space on the weak side of the opposition.

CHAPTER 5

The Transition from Defence to Attack in the Middle Zone

The Transition from Defence to Attack in the Middle Zone

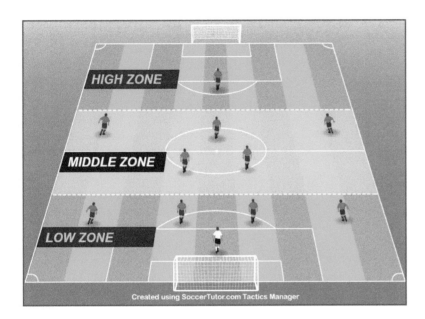

In this phase Spain scored a total of 8 goals in the 2008- 2012 period.

They scored in this phase in the first group match of Euro 2008 against Russia, 4 in the qualifiers for the World Cup and 1 in their third group game at the finals in 2010.

Spain also scored 1 goal in the Euro 2012 qualifiers and 1 at the finals.

There were 2 key points (similarities) in all of these goals in this situation:

- The quick and quality first pass when the opposition were unbalanced in defence and left free space in behind. There was great synchronisation between the passer and the player running into space.

- The very quick dribbling of the ball from the second player who normally receives from the player who wins the ball. This occurred when the opposition moved backwards or there were large distances between the opposition players or space in behind the defensive line.

In this situation the player dribbles the ball forward and up to the opposition while other teammates check away from their markers and run forward (and in behind the defensive line) to provide support.

The attack can continue and finish with good combination play (movements and cooperation we work on in the practices). Spain's players were very good at recognising the situation and would display good decision making, especially from the ball carrier and the player who played the final ball.

GOAL ANALYSIS

Quick Counter Attack in a 2 v 2 Situation with Curved Outside Run

10-Jun-2008: European Championship 2008 Qualifying

Spain 4-1 Russia (1st Goal): Villa - Assist: Torres

Spain in a 4-1-3-2 vs Russia in a 4-4-2

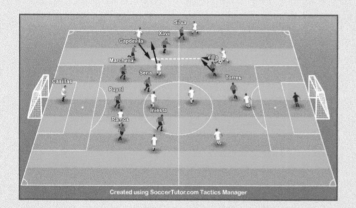

Russia are in possession and their 2 centre backs are marked by 2 attackers (Torres and Villa). The other 8 Spanish players display good defensive organisation.

The Russian defender is pressurised by Villa. 2 of his teammates make opposite movements (1 inside & 1 outside) and he tries to pass to the incoming player.

Capdevila reads the situation and gets to the ball first.

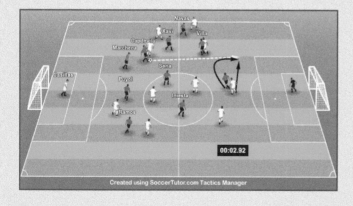

At the same time that the ball is travelling, Capdevila recognises the situation and makes a quick decision.

Capdevila passes with his first touch into the free space high up the pitch.

The ball is put into an area Torres has moved into who now has a 1v1 situation with one of the centre backs.

Torres (in a 1v1) takes the ball to the outside of the opponent and Villa makes a run in the opposite direction into the penalty area.

Villa provides support and gives another solution for Torres.

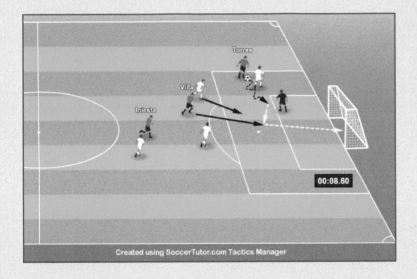

Torres dribbles inside his opponent and into the penalty area.

He now has more choices and at the correct time he passes to Villa who runs in from behind to meet the pass.

Villa finishes with 1 touch and makes it 1-0.

The attack was completed in 8.6 seconds from the time Capdevila intercepted the ball.

SESSION FOR THIS TOPIC *(7 Practices)*

1. Curved Outside Run to Receive in Behind

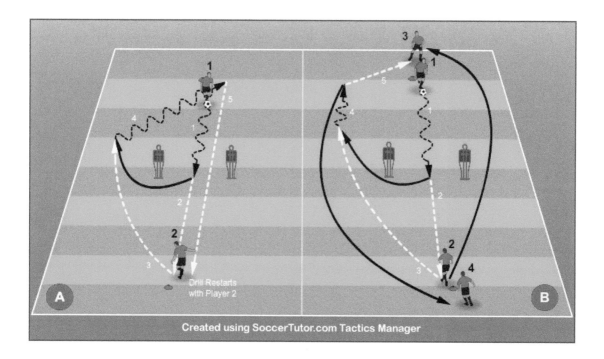

Objective

To develop the movement to check away from a marker, quick combination play and running with the ball.

Description

A) We work in pairs inside an area 15 yards in length. We place 2 mannequins in the middle with 2 yards distance between them.

Player 1 starts by dribbling with the ball and before he reaches the mannequin, he passes the ball to player 2. Player 2 plays a 1 touch pass to player 1 to the left or right (depending on which side Player 1 has made the movement round the mannequin as shown).

Player 1 receives and dribbles back to the starting position. Then player 1 passes to player 2 and player 2 repeats the drill starting from the opposite side.

B) We work in the same way but now with 4 players. This time player 1 does not dribble all the way back to the starting position but instead dribbles, passes to Player 3 and then runs to the other side. Player 2 runs to the other side after his 1 touch pass.

This 4 man drill works on a continuous loop and the sequence does not include a change of direction. The coach can stop the drill and change the direction when they see fit.

VARIATION
2. Curved Outside Run to Receive in Behind (2)

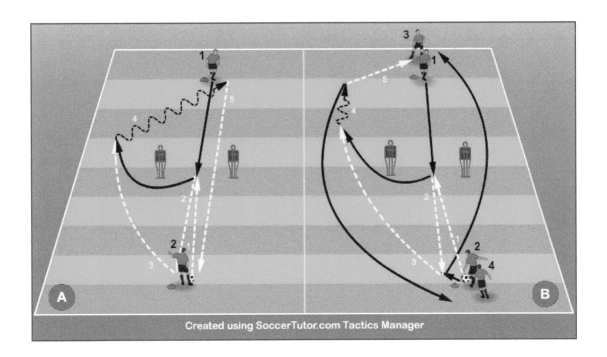

Created using SoccerTutor.com Tactics Manager

Description

A) This time player 1 starts without the ball and runs up to the mannequins to receive a pass from player 2 and plays a pass straight back to him and then makes the curved outside run (to the left or right of the mannequins). Player 2's second pass is into to the space player 1 has run into.

Player 1 receives and dribbles back to the starting position. Then player 1 passes to player 2 and player 2 starts the drill from the other side.

B) We work in the same way but now with 4 players. This time player 1 does not dribble all the way back to the starting position but instead dribbles, passes to Player 3 and then runs to the other side. Player 2 runs to the other side after his second pass.

This 4 man drill works on a continuous loop and the sequence does not include a change of direction. The coach can stop the drill and change the direction when he or she sees fit.

Coaching Points

1. The correct body shape should be monitored (opening up) and receiving/passing with the back foot (foot furthest away from the ball).
2. Use the part of the foot suitable for the distances in each part of the drill and the players must anticipate the next movement to make it flow.
3. Accuracy of pass, weight of pass and good communication are all key elements for this practice.

PROGRESSION

3. Attacking Combination Play with Inside / Outside Runs

A

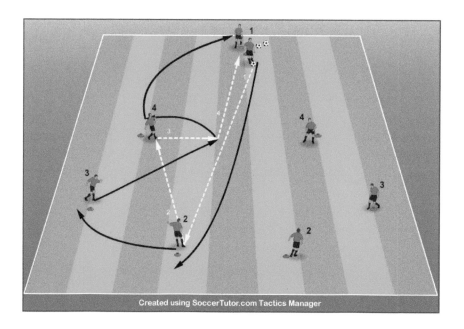

B

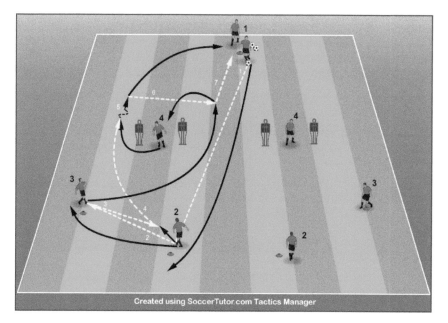

Description

A) We have 8 players in 7 marked positions (on cones as shown) playing a passing sequence.

Player 1 starts by passing to player 2. Player 2 passes to player 4 and while the ball is travelling, player 3 makes a cutting run inside. Player 4 passes to player 3 and player 3 passes back to the starting position to the next player waiting.

The drill then continues the same way from the other direction. All players move along 1 position (1 to 2, 2 to 3 etc).

B) Now we progress the drill and put 2 mannequins in position 4 on both sides as shown.

Player 1 passes the ball to player 2. Player 2 passes to player 3 who passes straight back to him. Player 2 then passes into the space (outside of the mannequins) where player 4 has made a quick unmarking movement (curved outside run).

Player 4 receives the ball, dribbles forward and passes to Player 3 who has made a curved run around the 2 mannequins. Player 3 receives and passes back to the starting position for the next player waiting.

The drill continues the same way in the other direction. All players move along 1 position (1 to 2, 2 to 3 etc).

Coaching Points

1. These sequences can be done with 1-2 touches or 1 touch only.
2. Passes need to be very accurate and timed to movement/run of their teammates.
3. Use the part of the foot suitable for the distances in each part of the drill and the players must anticipate the next movement to make it flow.

SPAIN Attacking Sessions

PROGRESSION

4. Attacking Combination Play with Curved Outside Run and Shot

Created using SoccerTutor.com Tactics Manager

Description

For this progression we add a full sized goal with a goalkeeper.

The drill starts with the goalkeeper who passes the ball to player 1. Player 1 passes to player 3 into the space where he has made the unmarking movement. Player 3 receives, dribbles forward and passes to player 2 who has made an inside cutting run at the correct time.

Player 2 shoots first time on goal. The drill continues from the other side. All players move to the next position and the drill runs from both sides.

Coaching Points

1. The timing of player 3's movement is the key to the rhythm of this passing combination.
2. Accuracy of pass, weight of pass and good communication are all key elements for this practice.

PROGRESSION

5. Inside & Outside Attacking Runs with 2 v 1 Duel and Finishing

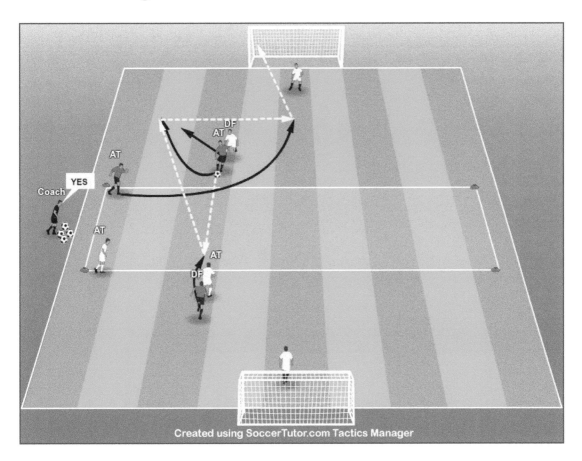

Created using SoccerTutor.com Tactics Manager

Description

In an area 50 x 25 yards we have 2 full sized goals and a zone marked out in the middle (10 yards long).

The players start in the positions shown in the diagram. 2 attackers exchange passes and all the players wait for the coach's signal.

While the ball is travelling from one attacker to another, the coach can give his signal ('YES' in diagram) and the defender can run in front of him and passes into space for his attacker. The other attacker from the side makes an inside (curved) opposite run and we have a 2v1 situation in front of the goal.

When the attack is finished, the players swap sides and run the practice again (or we have 6 players on the other side).

Rule

The attack must finish within a set amount of time (e.g. 6 seconds).

209

PROGRESSION

6. Transition to Attack in the Middle Zone with a Curved Run & Pass Out Wide in a 7 v 7 Dynamic 3 Zone Small Sided Game

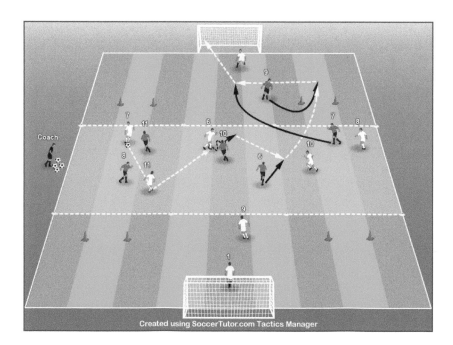

Objective

We work on keeping possession, winning the ball and playing a quick pass out wide for a curved run and finishing the attack.

Description

In an area 60 x 30 yards, we divide the pitch into 3 zones (20 x 30 yards each). In the central zone we have a 5v5 situation and each team has 4 midfielders and 1 attacker from the 4-1-3-2 (or 4-4-2) and in the final zone each team has an additional attacker. We also place 8 cones in the positions shown to create 2 gates for each attacker.

The game starts with one team in possession as they aim to complete 6-8 passes before passing to their attacker in the final zone. If this is achieved, then all players can move into the final zone to attack/defend but the attacker is not allowed to shoot unless a teammate has touched the ball within the final zone already.

The objective for the defending team is to win the ball and move into a quick transition to attack. 1 player can move forward from the central zone and the attacker passes across to them for a first time finish (as shown in diagram). When passing into the final zone, it has to be through the gate where the attacker has made their movement.

Rules

1. At the beginning when the team goes into transition to attack, the defenders are not allowed to enter the final zone (progress to 1 defender being allowed in the final zone).

2. All players in the central zone have unlimited touches (or 2-3 touches).

3. When a team wins the ball in the central zone, the ball must get to the final zone within 4 seconds or the ball is given back to the other team.

4. The attackers are limited to 2 touches in the final zone.

PROGRESSION

7. Transition to Attack in the Middle Zone with a Curved Run & Pass Out Wide in a Dynamic 3 Zone Game

Description

On a full sized pitch we put 1 goal on the edge of the box and create 3 zones. The whites are in a 4-1-4-1 formation and the reds/blues are in a 4-1-3-2. It is 9v9 in the central zone and 1v1 in the high zone.

The defending team have 6 red players and 3 blue. The blue players are the only ones who are allowed to move into the final zone when the team goes into transition to attack (LM, RM & CM or 2nd striker).

The white team start in possession and try to score. The red & blues defend from within the central zone. If the white team can pass the ball into the end zone, no red/blue players can follow, but they have limited time or touches to finish their attack.

The objective for the red team is to win the ball in the central zone and pass quickly to the attacker in the high zone (in the space left or right of him). If this happens, one of the 3 blue players can move into the high zone to support the attacker. 1 white player is also allowed to move into the final zone to defend. After, progress to all players being allowed in the final zone.

Rules

1. The white team have unlimited touches in the central zone and 2 touches in zone 1.

2. The red/blue players are limited to 2 touches in the central zone and have unlimited touches in the high zone.

3. The blue players must finish with 1 touch.

4. The reds have 4 seconds to pass the ball into the high zone and 10 seconds to finish their attack.

GOAL ANALYSIS

Winning the Ball in the Middle Zone, Quick Pass and Counter Attack

05-Sep-2009: World Cup 2010 Qualifying

Spain 5-0 Belgium (1st Goal): Silva - Assist: Villa

Spain in a 4-4-2 vs Belgium in a 4-2-3-1

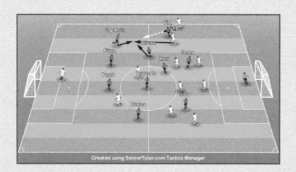

The Belgian right back dribbles forward up against Villa and passes to the right midfielder who makes a forward run in between Villa and Alonso.

Capdevila and Alonso press him and win the ball, before passing to Villa on the left.

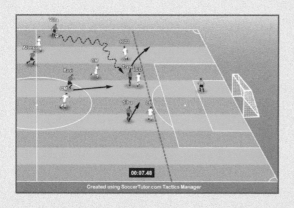

Villa has the ball and Spain make a positive transition with 3 (+1) teammates vs 3 (+2) opponents.

Villa dribbles inside as Torres makes an opposite run to the left of him and Xavi runs from deep to provide support to him. Silva moves inside from the right side.

Torres wants the ball played into space, Xavi wants it to feet and Silva wants the ball in behind the defence. Villa has 3 good passing options.

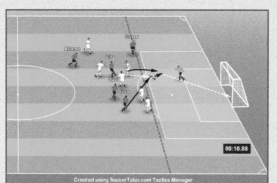

2 Belgian defenders move to close down Villa and they leave free space behind them.

Silva makes a diagonal cutting run into the area. Villa passes to him into this space at the correct time and Silva controls the ball and scores.

This attack took 10.88 seconds.

212

SESSION FOR THIS TOPIC *(6 Practices)*

1. GROUP A: Winning the Ball & Quick Pass in a Continuous 3 Zone Gauntlet Game

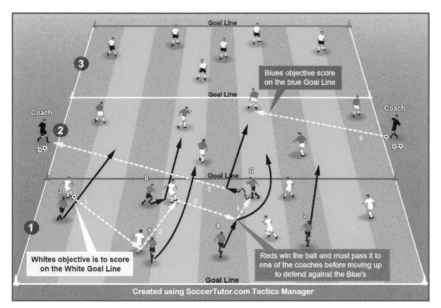

Objective

We work on winning the ball, quickly passing to start a counter attack, maintaining possession & passing in behind the defensive line.

Competition

This is a 4 team game where points are scored (1 for winning the ball and passing to coach / 2 for getting in behind defensive line).

Which team will score the most points?

Description

In an area 75 x 40 yards we divide the pitch into 3 equal zones (25 x 40 yards). We have 4 teams of 6 players. In the first zone we have the red team in a 4-2 formation (4 defenders & 2 centre midfielders) against a white team in possession with a 2-3-1 (from 4-2-3-1) or 4-2 / 4-1-1.

The objective for the white team is to get past the end line in behind the red defensive line (dribbling or receiving a pass in behind - 2 points). The objective for the reds it is to use good ball oriented defence and win the ball from the whites. If this happens, they then pass to a coach on either side of the middle zone (1 point).

The reds then move quickly to the next grid as a coach passes a new ball to the blue team. The blues aim to get in behind the red's defensive line and the reds have the same objective as they did in the first zone.

If the reds are successful again, the drill continues with the reds moving to zone 3 to win the ball from the yellows. If they win the ball this time, they try to get past the final end line in behind the yellow defensive line.

If a team gets in behind the defensive line of their opponents without losing the ball, they score 1 point. When the red's attack finishes (they lose the ball or get past the last goal line) all teams changes roles. Here the white team would start the drill defending against the blues in zone 1, vs yellow in zone 2 and vs red in zone 3.

Rules

1. From the moment a teams wins the ball, they have 5 seconds to pass the ball to a coach.
2. All attackers have unlimited (or 2-3) touches.

PROGRESSION
2. GROUP A: Winning the Ball & Quick Pass in a Continuous 3 Zone Gauntlet Game with Goals

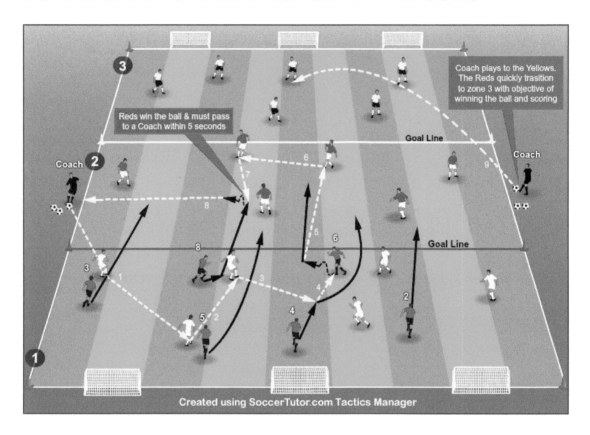

Coach plays to the Yellows. The Reds quickly trasition to zone 3 with objective of winning the ball and scoring

Reds win the ball & must pass to a Coach within 5 seconds

Goal Line

Coach

Goal Line

Created using SoccerTutor.com Tactics Manager

Description

Using the same area we now put 3 mini goals at each end. In zone 1 the reds defend the 3 mini goals, in zone 2 they must stop the blues dribbling past the line and in zone 3 they must stop the opposition passing into the middle zone (yellow to blue in this diagram).

When the reds win the ball in zone 1, they pass to the blues and run up very quickly to defend against them. When they win the ball in zone 2, they must pass to a coach at the side within 5 seconds. Immediately, the other coach passes a long ball to the yellow attacking team in zone 3.

The red team must run quickly again to defend against the yellows. If the reds win the ball in zone 3, the objective is to score in 1 of the 3 mini goals. When the reds attack finishes (they score or the ball goes out of play) all teams change roles as in the previous practice.

Rules

1. The same rules as the previous drill.
2. In zone 3 the attack must finish within 10 seconds and the players have unlimited touches to do so.

3. GROUP B: Dribbling the Ball Inside to Create Passing Options in Behind the Defensive Line (4-4-2 / 4-4-1-1 Pattern of Play)

Created using SoccerTutor.com Tactics Manager

Objective

We work on a pattern of play where the ball carrier dribbles inside and the others make runs in behind the defensive line to receive a through ball. This develops dribbling and the timing of the final run to the final ball.

Description

In an area 50 x 40 yards we have a full sized goal (with goalkeeper), 5 mannequins in the positions shown and mark out a line 18 yards from the goal (same distance as penalty area). We work with 5 players (centre midfielder, left midfielder, right midfielder and 2 attackers).

The goalkeeper plays a long ball to the centre midfielder (6). This player must control well and pass immediately to the left midfielder (11). No.11 receives and uses the same movement as shown in the goal analysis (against Belgium). He dribbles inside and the others make the specific runs shown in the diagram. The ball carrier has 3 options to pass in behind and we leave the decision making to him.

For option 1, the other wide midfielder (7) receives in the middle, in option 2 the striker (9) receives on the left and No.7 runs to the near post, 10 to the far post and 11 runs in from the back. Finally, if option 3 is chosen, a 1-2 combination is played with the attacking midfielder (10) before shooting.

If the goalkeeper starts by passing to the other centre midfielder (8), he passes to the right midfielder (7) who dribbles inside and the players on the left make the same runs as their teammates did, but from the opposite side.

PROGRESSION
4. GROUP B: Dribbling the Ball Inside to Create Passing Options in Behind the Defensive Line in a 6 v 5 Zonal Game

Objective
We work on a specific tactical movement within a 5v6 zonal game (dribble inside & pass in behind defensive line).

Description
We again have 3 zones and put 2 small goals at one end and a full sized goal at the other end. The zone with 2 mini goals is 10 x 40 yards, the middle zone is 30 x 40 yards and the third zone is 18 x 40 yards. We have 5 white defenders (3 in the middle zone & 2 in the high zone of the white team).

The goalkeeper starts and plays a long ball to the final zone (where the 2 red centre midfielders are). 2 white players try to press the ball and to block any passes to the left or right midfielder. If the whites win the ball in this zone, they try to score in the 2 mini goals.

If the reds manage to pass to the middle zone, the 4 players in there launch an attack with a 4 v 3 (+1 white who returns from the low zone). The aim is to play a ball in behind the defensive line for a teammate to score using the same tactical movements from the previous pattern of play.

Rules
1. No other players can enter the low zone in the first phase. It is just a 2v2 situation.
2. If the white team win the ball in zone 2, we change to play a normal small sided game.
3. The 2 red centre midfielders have unlimited touches and when the ball goes into the middle zone, the red team's attack must finish within 8-10 seconds.

216

PROGRESSION
5. GROUP A & B: Winning the Ball in the Middle Zone & Passing Immediately in Behind (Position Specific 8 v 8 Game)

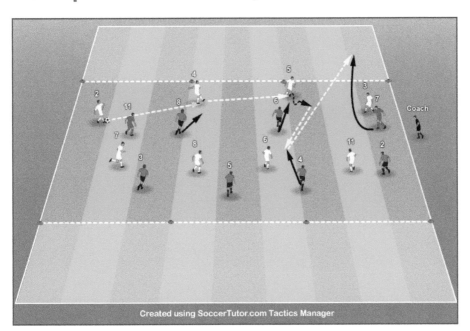

Created using SoccerTutor.com Tactics Manager

Objective
We work on winning the ball in the middle zone and passing immediately in behind the defensive line.

Description
In an area 75 x 55 yards we have 3 zones again. The middle zone is 55 x 55 yards and the 2 end zones are 10 x 55 yards. We have 2 teams of 8 players both in a 4-4 formation. The 4 defenders and the 2 centre midfielders have the same colour shirts and the wide midfielders on both sides wear a different colour.

The aim is to use a ball oriented defence and prevent the opposition from playing into the final zone and in behind the defensive line. If a team wins the ball they make a quick transition to attack by immediately passing in behind the opposition at the other end. Only the wide midfielders (blue/yellow) can receive in the end zones.

Rules
1. The team in possession can score either by dribbling into or passing to a teammate into (and controlling the ball within) the end zone.
2. The team in possession have unlimited touches and the team who go into transition are limited to 2-3 touches.
3. The team in possession have unlimited time to complete their attack and the team who go into transition have a limited time to attack (8 seconds).

PROGRESSION
6. GROUP A & B: Winning the Ball in the Middle Zone & Quick Counter Attack in a 5 Zone Game on a Full Pitch

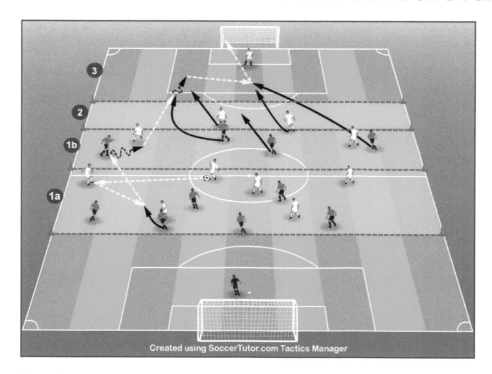

Created using SoccerTutor.com Tactics Manager

Objective
We work on winning the ball in the middle zone and quickly attacking in the final third (in behind defence).

Description
Using a full pitch we create a middle defensive zone and divide it into 1a and 1b. We also create another line 10 yards outside the white's penalty area. The white team are in a 4-2-3-1 formation and the red team are in a 4-4-2 formation with a bowl.

The game starts with the white goalkeeper and the white team aim to keep possession and score a goal at the opposite end. The red team starts to defend when the ball enters the middle zone (1b).

If the red team win the ball in area 1b, they can go into transition to attack and try to use the same combinations and movements we worked on in the previous practices. If the red team win the ball in area 1a, they must pass the ball to their teammates in area 1b, before then attacking in the same way.

Rules
1. The white defenders are not allowed in zone 3 before the ball is played in there.
2. White players have unlimited touches.
3. The red players have 2 touches in areas 1a & 3 and unlimited touches in areas 1b and 2.
4. If the reds win the ball in zone 1a, they must finish the attack within 10-12 seconds.
5. If the reds win the ball in zone 1b, they must finish the attack within 8-10 seconds.
6. The red players in defence are not allowed to enter the low zone (behind them) before the white team pass the ball into this zone.

218

GOAL ANALYSIS

Creating a Numerical Advantage in the Centre & Quick Counter Attack using the Flank

05-Sep-2009: World Cup 2010 Qualifying

Spain 5-0 Belgium (3rd Goal): Pique - Assist: Villa

Spain in a 4-4-2

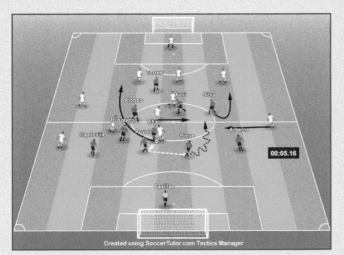

Belgium are attacking but Spain have a numerical superiority around the ball.

Villa sprints back to press the opponent who loses the ball and it falls to Puyol.

Puyol passes to Pique who has free space in front of him.

Pique dribbles the ball forward which creates a numerical advantage in the centre of the pitch.

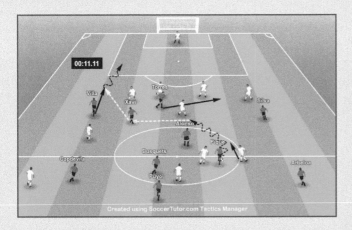

Pique passes the halfway line in between the 2 opponents and creates a 5 (+1) v 5 situation in the final third.

The opposition's defensive line is close to the edge of the penalty area. Pique dribbles up to the opponent and then passes to Xavi on the left.

Xavi passes very quickly to Villa (who has made a fast run forward after pressurising the ball before) into the free space on the left.

Villa dribbles the ball into the box.

Villa has 2 defenders in front of him and one of them moves to press Villa and the second covers the first defender.

Torres makes a run to the near post and takes the centre back with him.

Pique continues his run into the penalty area and calls for the ball.

Villa passes to him.

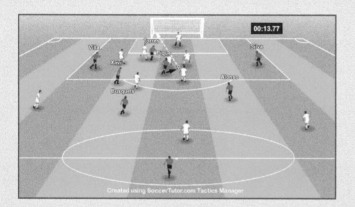

Pique takes a good directional first touch to his right and finishes well into the corner, opposite to the movement of the goalkeeper.

The attack took 13.77 seconds.

SESSION FOR THIS TOPIC *(4 Practices)*

1. Break through the Centre, Pass to the Flank, Support Play & Finishing Practice

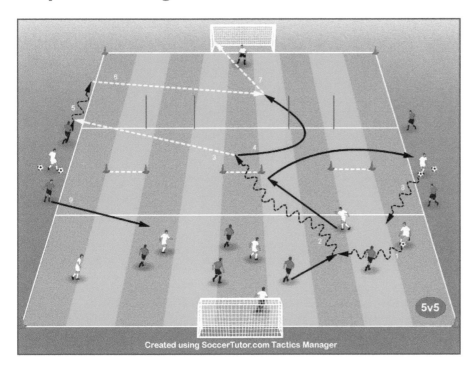

Objective

To develop quick dribbling through the centre, passing into space and timing runs into the penalty area.

Description

In an area 60 x 40 yards, divide the pitch into 3 zones (20 x 40 yards each). We have 2 full sized goals with goalkeepers and 6 large cones in the middle to create 3 gates. We also have 4 poles which create another 2 gates.

In the first zone we have a 5v5 situation and at the sides we have 2 white players with a ball each, 2 red defenders and 2 red attackers. The white team try to score in the goal and the 5 reds must defend the goal with the objective to win the ball and move into a transition to attack with a player dribbling past the first line.

If a red player passes the first line, only 1 white player can follow into the middle zone to try and stop them dribbling through 1 of the 3 gates. If the red player dribbles the ball through one of the gates, the white player stops defending. Now the red player passes the ball to the left or right (red attackers on the outside) and makes an opposite run through the poles. The side player crosses the ball for him to finish on goal.

At the moment the red player dribbles through the cones, another white player from the side enters with a new ball (the white defender goes out) and 1 red player from the side comes inside as defender and we start again with a 5v5 situation in the first zone.

Coaching Points

1. The dribbling part should be done at high speed to drive away from the opponent (fast break attack).
2. The cross needs to be with the correct weight and the run into the final zone needs to be well timed.

PROGRESSION

2. Quick Counter Attack, Crossing & Finishing with Wide Support Players in a 5 v 5 (+4) Transition Game

PART 1

PART 2

Objective

To develop fast break attacks with good attacking combination play - quick dribbling through the centre, passing into space and timing runs into the penalty area.

Description

In an area 50 x 25 yards we put 2 mini goals at each end. We have a 5v5 game (+4 neutral players in the positions shown in part 1).

The game starts in one half with one team (+2 neutrals) in possession (white in the diagram).The red team defend the 2 mini goals and if they win the ball, their objective is to counter attack using the neutral players and to score in the 2 mini goals at the opposite end.

The red team then start with possession and the 4 neutral players must change their positions as shown in the second diagram (part 2).

Rules

1. All inside players are limited to 3 touches (progress to 2 touches).
2. The neutral players are limited to 1 touch.

Coaching Points

1. Runs to meet the final cross/pass should be coordinated with teammates (1 to each goal & 1 behind) to replicate near/far post runs and running in from the back on a full pitch.
2. The counter attack should be done at high pace with all players moving forward to support.
3. Quick and quality final balls and finishing should be monitored.

PROGRESSION

3. Quick Counter Attack, Crossing & Finishing with Wide Support Players in a 2 Zone Small Sided Game

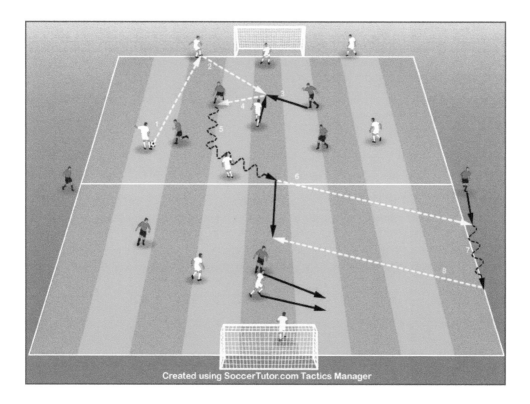

Created using SoccerTutor.com Tactics Manager

Objective

We work on winning the ball with a numerical disadvantage and launching a quick counter attack out wide.

Description

We now have an 8v8 game with 2 full sized goals and goalkeepers. The white team have 4 players (+2 outside at the end) in the opposition half and 2 players in their own half. The red team have 4 players defending in their own half, 2 in the opposition half and 2 support players outside on the left and right.

The 4 red players try to protect their goal first and win the ball. Their second objective is to launch a fast break attack. Only 1 player (by dribbling forward) can move into the opposition half. The red team have a 3 v 2 (+2) situation to finish their attack and should use the wide support players.

Rules

1. The white attackers (4 [+2 at the ends] in this case) are not allowed to track back to their own half.
2. In the reds transition to attack all players are limited to 2-3 touches.
3. The side players are limited to 2 touches.
4. Limit the time for the team in transition to finish their attack (e.g. 8 seconds).

224

PROGRESSION

4. Quick Counter Attack, Crossing & Finishing with Wide Support Players in an 11 v 11 Game on a Full Pitch

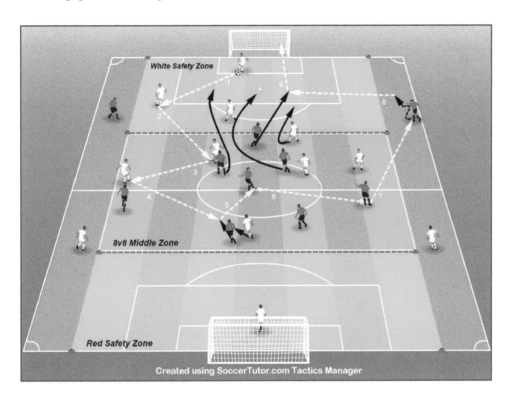

Created using SoccerTutor.com Tactics Manager

Description

Using a full pitch we now have an 11v11 situation. We create 3 zones (1 central zone and 2 final zones). Both teams have 8 players in the central zone and 2 outside players at the sides in each corner as shown.

One team starts with the ball (white in the diagram) and attacks in a 4-2-3-1 formation. When in possession in the 'White Safety Zone', no red players are allowed to enter. The reds start their defence in the middle zone.

The 2 outside players at the sides only play as support players. They are not allowed to enter any of the 3 zones.

The red team defend in a 4-4-2 formation and try to win the ball. If they do, they pass quickly to one of the outside wide players who only play in the transition phase and pass/cross to players running from the central zone. Once the reds have possession, all their players are allowed to enter the 'White Safety Zone' to finish.

Rules

1. The team in transition have 10-12 seconds to finish their attack from the time they win the ball.
2. The players at the sides (outside) are limited to 2 touches.
3. All players have unlimited touches in the middle zone and 2 touches in the end zones
4. When a team wins the ball in the middle zone, they must pass to the side players within 4-6 seconds.

225

GOAL ANALYSIS

Quick Pass in Behind the Defensive Line after Regaining Possession (1)

05-Sep-2009: World Cup 2010 Qualifying

Spain 5-0 Belgium (5th Goal): Villa - Assist: Fabregas

Spain in a 4-4-2 vs Belgium in a 4-2-3-1

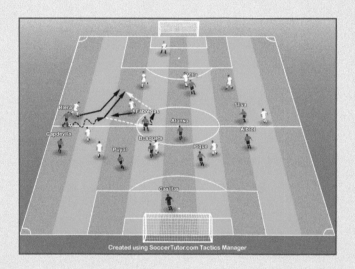

Spain are in possession and Riera dribbles inside from the left and plays a 1-2 combination with Fabregas in the centre.

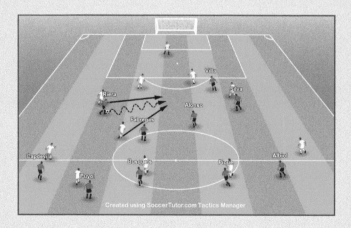

Riera receives the ball back and continues to dribble inside, but he loses the ball after being put under pressure by 2 opponents.

226

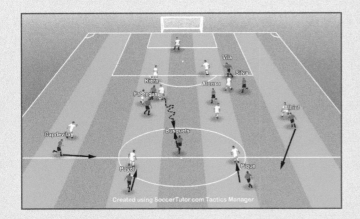

Now Spain goes from attack to defence (negative transition) and all players have moved inside. The 2 centre backs move forward and close the distances between them and their direct opponents. The 2 full backs move back and inside.

The opponent tries to move forward quickly by dribbling the ball, but Busquets moves up to press him.

The first objective is to stop the opponent dribbling forward and the second is to limit his options to pass to his teammates.

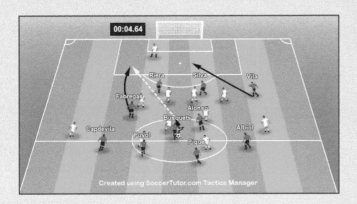

Busquets shows good positioning and anticipation to win the ball. Now Spain make a positive transition.

The opposition's defensive organisation is not good and Fabregas makes a run in behind the left back.

Busquets passes into the space in front of Fabregas. Villa also makes a run from the other side into the penalty area.

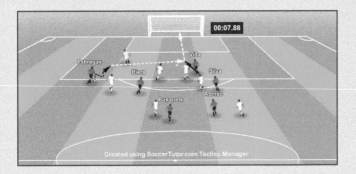

Fabregas receives on the edge of the box and when the goalkeeper sprints out to close him down, he passes to Villa who is in a better position. Villa taps into an open net.

From the time that Busquets won the ball back to Villa scoring was 7.88 seconds.

SPAIN Attacking Sessions

GOAL ANALYSIS

Quick Pass in Behind the Defensive Line after Regaining Possession (2)

14-Oct-2009: World Cup 2010 Qualifying

Bosnia Hz 2-5 Spain (2nd Goal): Silva - Assist: Negredo

Spain in a 4-1-4-1 vs Bosnia Hz in a 4-1-3-2

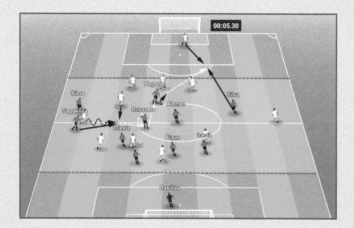

Spain are defending in the middle zone with good organisation. The opposition have the ball on Spain's left side and Capdevila is closest to the ball carrier.

Capdevila tackles the opponent and the ball falls to Busquets who passes very quickly to Negredo (the striker).

Negredo takes a very good directional first touch out in front of him. At the same time, Silva makes a run from the right side into the free space in behind the defensive line and receives a good pass from Negredo.

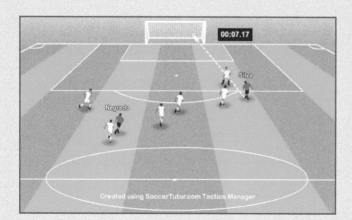

David Silva is faster than his opponent and gets to the ball first.

The goalkeeper runs out and Villa hits an excellent shot with the inside of his foot to score the goal.

The attack took 7.17 seconds.

GOAL ANALYSIS

Quick Pass in Behind the Defensive Line after Regaining Possession (3)

14-Jun-2012: European Championship 2012 Qualifying

Spain 4-0 Ireland (3rd Goal): Torres - Assist: Silva

Spain in a 4-3-3 vs Ireland in a 4-4-2

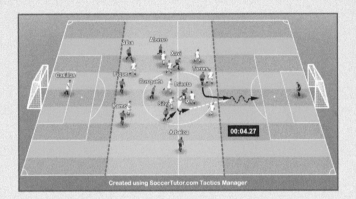

All outfield players from both teams are within the highlighted middle zone. Iniesta presses his opponent and the ball goes to Silva who notices that the opposition's defensive line is high and unbalanced.

Torres asks for the ball to be played into the free space in between the centre backs. Silva passes to him and now Torres has the advantage against the 2 defenders who chase him.

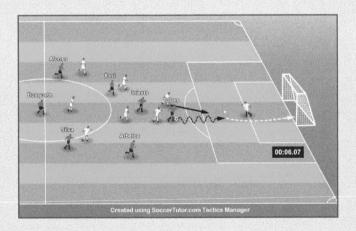

Torres dribbles the ball into the box and scores past the goalkeeper.

From the time that Silva took the ball, the attack was finished in 6.07 seconds.

SPAIN Attacking Sessions

SESSION FOR THIS TOPIC *(5 Practices)*

1. Regaining Possession Quickly in a Dynamic 12 v 7 Transition Game without Goalkeepers

Created using SoccerTutor.com Tactics Manager

Objective

We work on closing the time and space available for our opponents immediately after losing the ball and winning the ball back, as well as possession play.

Description

In an area 40 x 20 yards we have a game with 2 full sized goals without goalkeepers. The white team have 7 players all inside the playing area and the red team have 12 players (4 inside and 8 outside players) in the positions shown in the diagram.

The reds start in possession and their first objective is to complete 8 passes (1 point) or keep possession for 30 seconds (2 points). The second objective for the red team occurs when they lose possession (the whites win the ball). All players can enter the area and must very quickly close the space and press the opposition to prevent them from passing forward and scoring.

The reds must win the ball back within 6-8 seconds or the white team get 1 point and if the white team score a goal they get 2 points. If the reds win the ball back within 6-8 seconds, they try to keep possession again (to complete 8 passes) and the players take up their original positions. (We have the ball = Open the pitch, we lose the ball = Closed). If the whites score a goal (or the ball goes out of play), start the game from the beginning again.

Different Rules

1. The red outside players are limited to 2 touches and the inside players have unlimited touches.
2. The red outside players are limited to 1 touch and the inside players are limited to 2-3 touches.
3. The reds can only finish using 1 touch.
4. The white team have unlimited touches / The white team are limited to 2-3 touches.

SPAIN Attacking Sessions

PROGRESSION
2. Regaining Possession Quickly in a Dynamic 12 v 7 Transition Game with Goalkeepers & Passing Gates

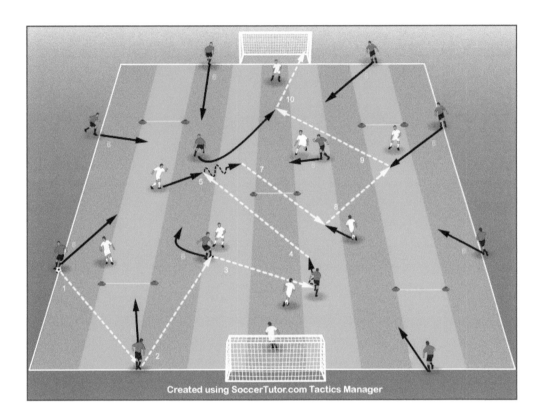

Created using SoccerTutor.com Tactics Manager

Description

This is the same as the previous practice, but now we add 5 cones (as shown in the diagram) and 2 goalkeepers.

The white team now have 2 more options if they win the ball from the reds. They can get 1 point each time a player passes to a teammate between the gates, 2 points if a white player dribbles the ball through a gate and 3 points if they score in either of the 2 goals.

The red team have the same objectives as before, but now their reaction to pressing the ball when losing possession must be done much quicker because there are 2 more options for the white team.

Coaching Points

1. The red players must close down the ball carrier very quickly and create a numerical advantage in the area around him (the ball zone) and prevent him passing the ball, dribbling with the ball or finishing on goal.
2. Players need good concentration and anticipation to recognise and react to the changing situation.

PROGRESSION
3. Regaining Possession and Fast Break Attack in a 9 v 9 Game

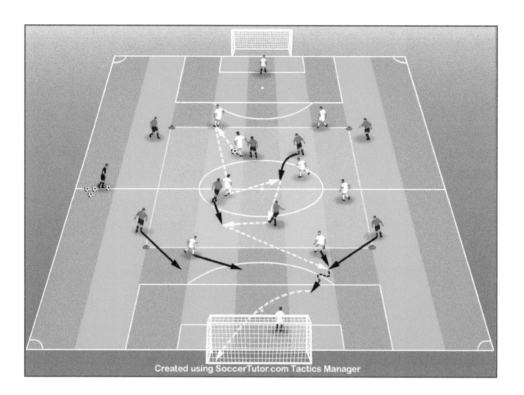

Created using SoccerTutor.com Tactics Manager

Objective

We work on the same aspects as previous 2 drills and now include fast combination play to finish counter attacks.

Description

We now progress and use a full pitch. The marked out zone in the centre is 32 x 32 yards.

We have an 8v8 situation with the outfield players and a goalkeeper at each end. 4 players from each team play Inside the central zone and the other 4 are positioned outside of the area (as shown in the diagram - 2 at opposite ends).

The white team's objective is to keep possession and they score 1 point if they complete 8 passes. The objective for the 4 red inside players is to apply pressure and win the ball. If they win the ball, they pass the ball to the outside players who try to score in either of the 2 goals. The white outside players defend the attack.

Coaching Points

1. The accuracy and weight of the final pass is key and needs to be timed for the run in behind.
2. The outside players need to respond quickly (anticipation & quick reactions) to the changing game situation so they get into the correct position to attack or defend.

232

SPAIN Attacking Sessions

VARIATION
4. Regaining Possession and Fast Break Attack in a 9 v 9 Game (2)

Description

We have the same objective as the previous drill, but now we change the starting positions of the outside players as shown in the diagram.

This now creates a 2v1 situation for the red team's counter attack.

Coaching Points

1. We use the same coaching points as the previous practice.
2. Encourage the players to use different attacking combinations, but every attack should be finished quickly (within 6-8 seconds).
3. We are looking for the players to dribble the ball at pace and demonstrate quality finishing.

PROGRESSION
5. Fast Break Attacks in a Dynamic 4 Zone 11 v 11 Transition Game

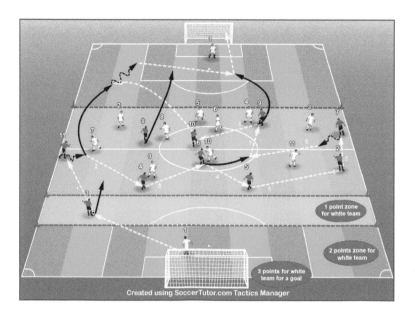

Created using SoccerTutor.com Tactics Manager

1 point zone for white team

2 points zone for white team

3 points for white team for a goal

Description

On a full pitch we play an 11v11 game with one team (red) in a 4-4-2 or 4-3-3 and another (white) in a 4-2-3-1 or 4-4-2. We have 2 scenarios in this practice.

Scenario 1

The attacks always start from the red goalkeeper. The red team attack from the back with the objective to complete 8 passes in the middle zone before then attacking in the final zone.

Completing 8 passes gets 1 point and if they score a goal they get 2 points (or more).

If the whites win the ball, they have 3 objectives. They win 1 point if they pass the ball into the small zone (just outside the penalty area), 2 points if they pass the ball into the final zone and 3 points if they score a goal. This helps the red team to improve how quickly and effectively they make their transition to defence. If the red team win the ball back in this phase of the game they have 6-8 seconds to finish their new attack.

Scenario 2

The attacks always start from the white goalkeeper. The white team have the same objective as the previous practice. The red team now start to press when it comes into the middle zone. If they win the ball they must make a very quick transition to attack and finish their attack within 6-8 seconds.

Rules for the 1st scenario

1. The red players have unlimited (or 3) touches in the middle zone and 2-3 touches in the other zones.
2. The white players have unlimited touches.
3. The white team start to press when the ball enters the middle zone.
4. While defending, the white players can defend in the final zone before the red team passes the ball in there.

Rules for the 2nd scenario

1. The red players are limited to 2-3 touches.
2. The white players have unlimited touches.
3. While defending, the white players can defend in the final zone before the red team passes the ball in there.

234

GOAL ANALYSIS

Breaking from the Middle Zone: Exploiting the Weaknesses in the Opposition Defence

03-Sep-10: European Championship 2012 Qualifying

Liechtenstein 0-4 Spain (1st Goal): Torres - Assist: Iniesta

Spain in a 4-4-2 vs Liechtenstein in a 4-2-3-1

Spain have a good ball oriented defence and make it difficult for the ball carrier to play out from the right flank. This forces the pass into the centre.

Iniesta shows good anticipation to intercept the ball and pass quickly for a fast transition to attack.

Iniesta plays a one-two combination with Torres and dribbles forward with the ball.

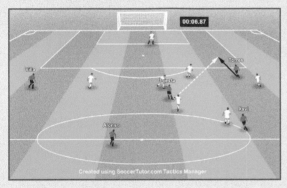

Iniesta has one option to his left with Villa and one to his right with Torres. The opposition defender's decision making and movements provide Iniesta with the solution.

There is a defensive imbalance on the right and Iniesta recognises the situation well and passes to Torres in the free space.

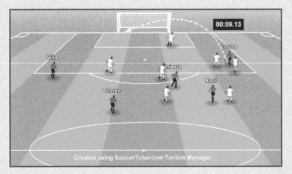

Torres displays excellent technique to chip the goalkeeper and score the goal.

The counter attack took 9.13 seconds.

235

SESSION FOR THIS TOPIC *(5 Practices)*

1. Fast Break Attack Game with 4 Different Scenarios

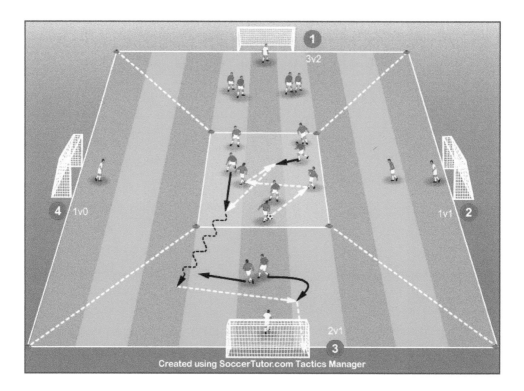

Created using SoccerTutor.com Tactics Manager

Objective

To develop possession play, winning the ball with a numerical disadvantage, fast break attacks and decision making.

Description

In an area 60 x 60 yards we have 4 goals (1 on each side) with 4 goalkeepers. In the middle we create a smaller square (15 x 15 yards). In this area we have 5 reds against 3 blue defenders in a rondo possession game.

Outside the square we have goal 1 with a 2v2 situation, goal 2 with 1 red defender, goal 3 with a 1v1 situation and finally goal 4 where we only have a goalkeeper.

The objective for the 3 defenders in the centre square is to win the ball and 1 player dribbles out of the square towards one of the 4 goals (progress later to being able to dribble or pass out of the square).

If the player chooses goal 1 there is a 3v2 situation, for goal 2 it is a 1v1, goal 3 is a 2v1 and goal 4 is a 1 on 1 with the goalkeeper.

Coaching Point

The players work to recognise games situations and to develop fast and quality decision making.

PROGRESSION

2. Possession & Fast Break Attack 3 Team Dynamic Transition Game

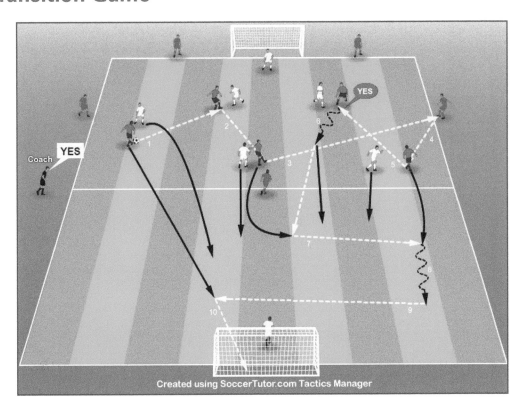

Created using SoccerTutor.com Tactics Manager

Objective

To develop fast break attacks with good decision making and support play (timing/weight of pass for forward runs).

Description

In an area 50 x 35 yards we divide into two 25 x 35 yard zones. We have 2 full sized goals with goalkeepers and 3 teams of 5 players each. The white team play against the reds and the blues are neutrals in the positions shown.

The objective of the game it is to keep possession of the ball (in one zone at a time) with the help of the neutrals who only play with the team in possession.

When the coach gives a signal, the team who has possession must attack the opposite goal in the other half very quickly (without help from the neutrals). After a few repetitions the teams should change roles.

Rules

1. In possession both teams play with unlimited touches and the neutrals are limited to 1 touch.
2. In the fast attacking phase the attackers are limited to 2-3 touches and must finish using 1 touch.

237

VARIATION

3. Possession & Fast Break Attack 3 Team Dynamic Transition Game (2)

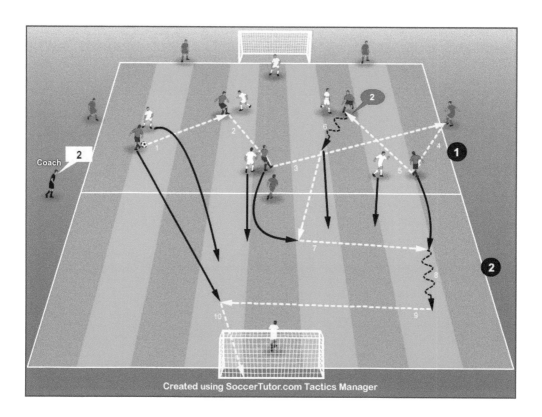

Created using SoccerTutor.com Tactics Manager

Description

In this variation we have now numbered the zones 1 and 2. The game starts in zone 1 with the same objectives and when the coach calls out '2' the team who has possession must attack in that zone.

In the case we have in the diagram, the red team must attack into an open pitch. If the coach calls out '1' the whites would have to attack in a closed pitch area (zone 1). The team in possession need to very quickly recognise the game situation and show good decision making.

Variation

If the coach calls out '1' then he can call out '2' a few seconds later to make the team go from a closed situation to attacking in an open situation very quickly to test their reactions.

Rules

The same as the previous practice, but when a team is attacking in a closed pitch they have unlimited touches.

PROGRESSION

4. Exploiting the Weaknesses in the Opposition Defence in a Dynamic 8 v 8 Small Sided Game

Created using SoccerTutor.com Tactics Manager

Objective

To develop player's vision, awareness and decision making so they are able to exploit the weaknesses (free space) in the opposition's defensive organisation for a quick counter attack.

Description

We use the same area again and play an 8v8 game. Each outfield player has a number from 1-7. When the ball goes out of play or a team loses possession, the coach calls out 2 numbers (in the diagram - '1 & 7').

The numbers relate to the team who kicked the ball out of play or lose possession. The 2 players called out must stop and stay in their positions and are not allowed to continue playing until there is a new call from the coach.

The team which makes the transition to attack always plays with a numerical advantage (7v5) and must quickly recognise the weaknesses (space) to exploit and take advantage to score.

Rules

1. The players for the team which makes the transition to attack are limited to 3 touches (progress to 2 touches).
2. The team which makes the transition to attack must finish their attack within a limited amount of time.

PROGRESSION

5. Fast Break Attacks with Different Numerical Scenarios in an 11 v 11 Game

Description

On a full pitch we play an 11v11 game. The red team use a 4-4-2 formation and the whites use a 4-2-3-1 or 4-3-3. We play a normal game and focus on defending in the middle zone.

The coach waits for a player (or team) to win the ball from the opposition in the middle zone and gives a signal (in diagram - 'YES'). When this signal is given, all players behind the ball must stop. This creates a transition to attack where only the highlighted players in the diagram can participate (players in front of the ball).

The attacking players must recognize the situation quickly (5v5 in this example) and find the weakness in the opposition defence and exploit it.

We work with the same elements from the previous practices in this session. We want the player to dribble forwards and play a quick ball into space, followed by good combination play. All of this player's teammates should make runs into space and some in behind the defensive line (as shown) to finish the attack quickly.

Variation

You can allow an extra 2 players to participate from the team which is in transition to attack (in this example in the diagram it would create a 7v5 situation instead of 5v5).

CHAPTER 6

The Transition from Defence to Attack in the High Zone

The Transition from Defence to Attack in the High Zone

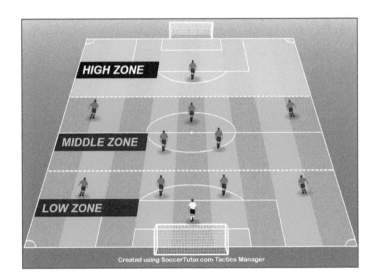

Spain scored 6 goals (2008-12) in the transition from defence to attack in the high zone.

For 3 of these goals Spain lost the ball in the high zone. There was a quick transition to defence with the objective to win the ball back again immediately again within the area they lost it.

Spain had a transition from attack to defence and then defence to attack (all within the high zone).

In this situation the nearest player presses the new ball carrier with the objective to prevent the player dribbling forwards or playing a quick pass to a teammate. The other players nearby apply a high press and close down the opponents nearest to the ball as the whole team squeezes the space.

The second and basic objective in this situation is that when Spain win the ball back, they go into a transition from defence to attack. They launch a fast attack and exploit any imbalance in the opposition's defensive line with 1 player making a run in behind. The player with the ball passes at the correct time into the space for him.

The other 3 goals started with the opposition in possession and Spain pressed high up the pitch. The objective in this situation was to apply a high press without committing a foul. The player who presses the ball carrier does not allow him space to dribble or pass to a teammate (especially in front). So the opponent is under pressure of space and time, and if he does not lose the ball himself, then the next player will after a poor pass.

In the cases when Spain won the ball back (transition to defence and transition to attack again) the objective is fast attacks like above. The first objective for the player who wins the ball is to pass to a teammate in a better position near to the opposition goal and produce quality and speed to finish the attack.

If there is nobody in a position like above, the player who has the ball creates this situation by dribbling forwards up to the opponents and uses the supporting runs of his teammates to pass to someone in a good position or exploit the space they create to shoot himself.

In both situations the attacks are normally concluded within 4-6 seconds (except for one situation when it took 8 seconds).

GOAL ANALYSIS

Transition from Attack to Defence & then Defence to Attack (1)

15-Sep-2008: World Cup 2010 Qualifying

Belgium 1-2 Spain (1st Goal): Iniesta - Assist: Fabregas

Spain in a 4-4-2 vs Belgium in a 4-1-4-1

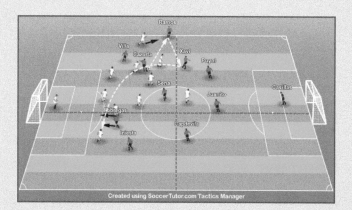

Spain have possession in the middle zone on the right and exchange passes.

Belgium push over to close down that side, Xavi plays a long ball to change the direction of play (and the rhythm) to the left and the weakest side of the opposition defensive line at that moment.

The ball is played in behind the defensive line into an area Fabregas is moving into, but the pass is not good and is blocked by the Belgian right back. He heads the ball to a centre midfielder in front of him.

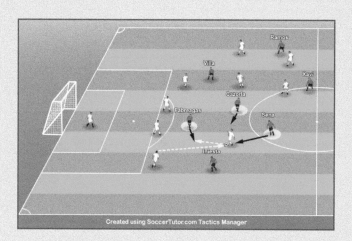

While the ball was travelling to the centre midfielder, Senna runs quickly to press the opponent from behind and the other Spanish players also close in around the ball carrier.

The Belgium centre midfielder makes a poor back pass and the ball is taken back by Fabregas.

244

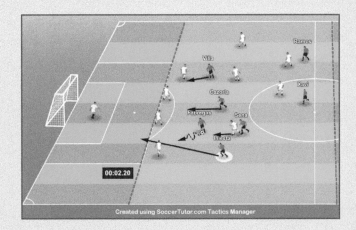

When Fabregas wins the ball, Iniesta quickly runs forward in front of Fabregas who is dribbling and asks for the ball to be played into the space between the full back and centre back.

The defensive line stays as one as the players do not leave their positions (not moving towards the ball or behind).

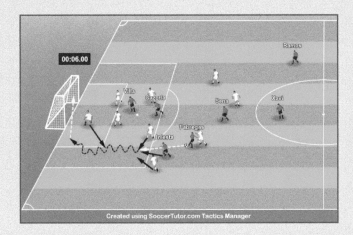

Fabregas passes at the correct time to Iniesta in the box and Iniesta has the advantage because he is running and the defenders are stationary.

Iniesta receives, shows great individual skill to take on the defenders and the goalkeeper and scores into an open net.

From the moment Spain won the ball back with Fabregas until Iniesta scored the goal, it took 6 seconds.

GOAL ANALYSIS

Transition from Attack to Defence & then Defence to Attack (2)

01-Jul-2012: European Championship 2012 Final

Spain 4-0 Italy (3rd Goal): Torres - Assist: Xavi

Spain in a 4-2-3-1 vs Italy in a 4-3-2 (with 10 players)

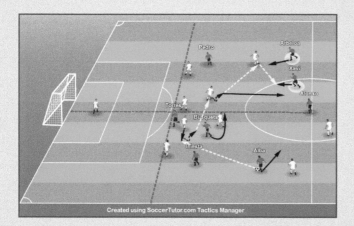

The same situation occurs against Italy in the Euro 2012 final. Spain have the ball and Alba tries to pass forward to Torres, but the Italian defender intercepts the ball. Immediately, the Spanish players nearby press him in this zone (in the grid shown).

The Italy defender is able to pass the ball to Pirlo in the next grid zone. Pirlo receives and tries to play a 1-2 with the left midfielder. Arbeloa and Xavi press them and Xavi anticipates the next pass and wins the ball back.

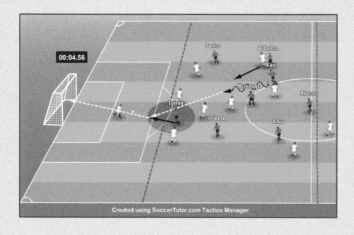

Xavi has free space in front and dribbles the ball forward.

Torres moves in between the 2 Italian defenders and in behind them.

Xavi passes at the correct time into the space for Torres.

Torres makes a simple but quality first touch finish and scores.

This attack took only 4.56 seconds.

SPAIN Attacking Sessions

GOAL ANALYSIS

Transition from Attack to Defence & then Defence to Attack (3)

14-Oct-2009: World Cup 2010 Qualifying

Bosnia Hz 2-5 Spain (3rd Goal): Mata - Assist: Silva

Spain in a 4-1-4-1 vs Bosnia Hz in a 4-1-3-2

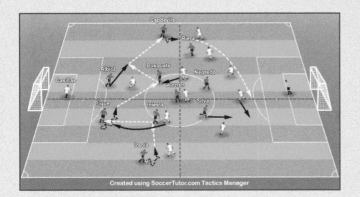

Spain are in possession. The attack starts with the right back (Iraola) and is worked with good synchronisation, short passing and support movements to the left back (Cepdevila).

Capdevila sees that the weak side of the opposition is now on the right, and with a long ball he tries to change the direction and rhythm of the attack.

Silva, the Bosnian centre back and the left back move into the area the long pass is played into.

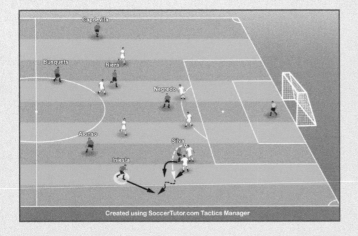

The Bosnian centre back heads the ball and the ball goes to the left back. Iniesta has sprinted forward and presses the left back, winning the ball from him.

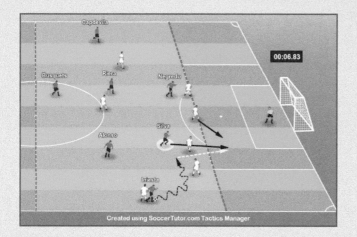

At this moment there is no Spanish player in the penalty area so Iniesta dribbles inside with the ball, creating time and space for his teammates to make support movements.

As Iniesta changes the direction of his dribbling and goes inside, Silva makes a run in between the 2 centre backs and in behind the back 4.

Iniesta passes at the correct time to Silva in the box.

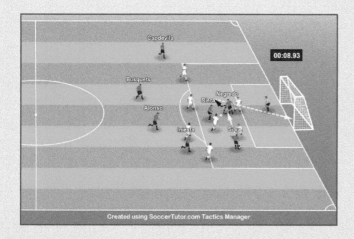

Silva makes a short cross to Negredo.

Negredo receives with his back to goal, produces an excellent turn and finishes in the opposite side of the net.

The attack was completed in 8.93 seconds.

SESSION FOR THIS TOPIC *(5 Practices)*

1. Continuous 6 v 5 Zonal Possession Game

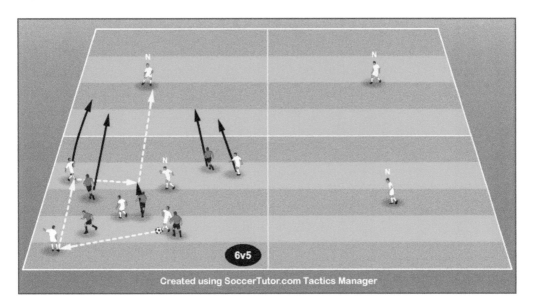

Objective

We work on keeping possession in small areas and quickly changing the direction of play.

Description

In an area 50 x 50 yards we create 4 zones (25 x 25 yards each). We have 2 teams of 5 players in one zone and 4 neutral players (1 in each zone).

The drill starts in one zone with the objective for the team in possession to complete 6 passes and then pass to a neutral player in another zone. All players then move to the next zone with the same objective again. After completing 6 passes and then changing zone the team scores 1 point. If they manage to move the ball through all 4 zones while keeping possession, the team scores 5 extra points.

If the defending team win the ball, they become the team in possession. They can either try to complete 6 passes within the same grid or pass to a neutral player in another grid, move across and try to complete 6 passes there.

Rules

1. The players and the ball can go from any grid to another without restriction.
2. All players have unlimited touches (or 2-3) and the neutral players are limited to 2 touches (or 1 touch).

Coaching Points

1. In tight spaces, the accuracy of the short passes is key to maintaining possession.
2. The correct body shape should be monitored (opening up) and receiving/passing with the back foot (foot furthest away from the ball).
3. This practice trains possession play and quickly switching the point of attack to the opposition's weak side.

PROGRESSION

2. Attack to Defence & then Defence to Attack in a Dynamic Transition Game with 4 Goals

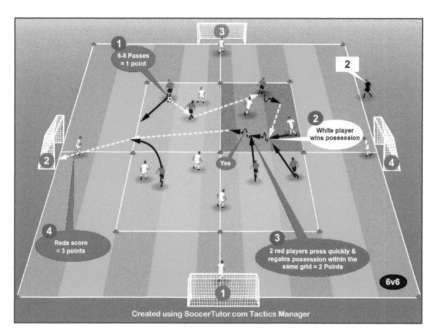

Objective

To develop possession play, winning the ball back quickly, quick reactions/awareness and finishing.

Description

We put a goal on each side of a 50 x 50 yard square with goalkeepers and number the goals 1-4. We also create another smaller square with 4 grids (15 yards x 15 yards each).

We play a 6v6 game within this area with the first objective to keep possession and complete 6-8 passes to get 1 point. When possession is lost, the second objective is to win the ball back very quickly again. If this happens within the same area they lost the ball they get 2 points.

Finally, the coach calls out a number (e.g. '2') which represents one of the 4 goals. The team which has just won the ball back then has the third objective to attack that numbered goal and if they score they get 3 points.

Variation

If one team has a problem attacking a specific goal, the coach can call out another number for the team to then attack (changing the point of attack very quickly).

Different Rules

1. All players have unlimited touches.
2. All players have unlimited touches in the 4 grids and 1-2 touches in front of the goals.
3. All players are limited to 2-3 touches in the 4 grids and 1 touch in front of the goals.

PROGRESSION

3. Transition from Attack to Defence & then Defence to Attack in a Dynamic 4 Zone Small Sided Game

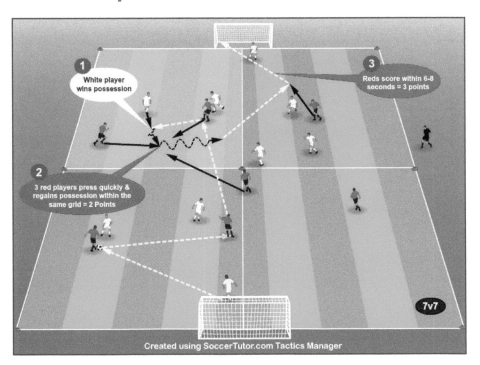

Created using SoccerTutor.com Tactics Manager

Description

In an area 50 x 50 yards we divide the pitch into 4 equal grids (25 x 25 yards) and have 1 full sized goal at each end. We play a normal 7v7 game and when a team scores they get 1 point.

The small sided game starts with one team in possession as they try to score. If they lose the ball, their objective is to then win the ball back quickly and make another transition back to attack.

If a team is able to win the ball back within the grid they lost the ball in they get 2 points. If they score within 6-8 seconds from the moment they win the ball back again they get 3 points.

Rules

1. All players have unlimited touches.
2. All players have unlimited touches in the normal game and 2-3 touches when making a transition from defence to attack.
3. All players are limited to 2-3 touches and goals must be scored with a 1 touch finish.

Coaching Points

1. The focus is on a quick transition to defence by pressing the opponent in the same area the ball is lost.
2. If the transition from defence to attack is achieved high up the pitch, the attack needs to be finished quickly.

PROGRESSION

4. Transition from Attack to Defence & then Defence to Attack in a Dynamic 5 Zone Small Sided Game

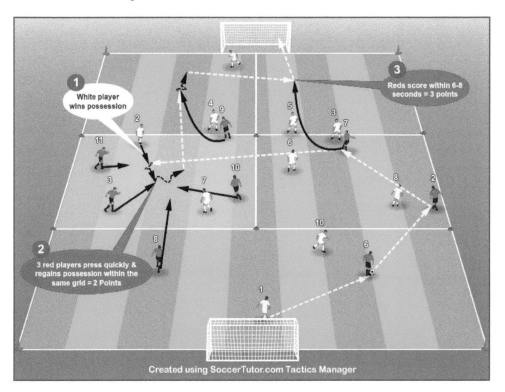

Created using SoccerTutor.com Tactics Manager

Description

In an area 45 x 30 yards we create 5 zones as shown in the diagram and play a 9v9 game. The red team are in a 2-2-3-1 formation (2FB, 2CM, 1 AM, 1 RM, 1 LM & 1 CF) and the white team are in a 4-4 with a diamond.

The game starts with the red goalkeeper and we play a free game with the focus on the red team when they lose possession. If they lose the ball, they should press in the high zone (the 4 grids) and try to get the ball back very quickly within the area they lose it. If they achieve this they get 2 points and if they score within 6-8 seconds from that moment they get 3 points.

If the reds score in normal play, they score 1 point and if the whites score at anytime they score 2 points.

Different Rules

1. All players have unlimited touches.
2. All players have unlimited touches but the red players are limited to 2-3 touches when they make a transition from defence to attack.
3. The white players have unlimited touches and the red players are limited to 2-3 touches.
4. The white players have unlimited touches and the red players are limited to 2-3 touches (and can only score with a 1 touch finish).

PROGRESSION

5. Transition from Attack to Defence & then Defence to Attack in a Dynamic 7 Zone Game on a Full Pitch

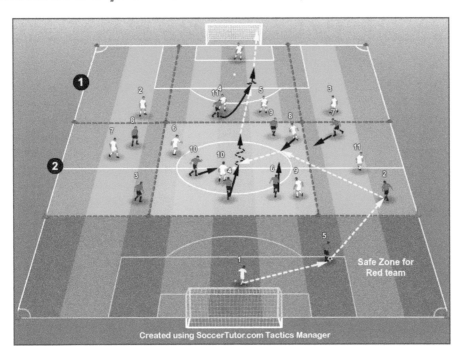

Created using SoccerTutor.com Tactics Manager

Description

We play an 11v11 game. We have 6 marked out zones and 1 safe zone for the red team in possession (as shown in the diagram). The red team are in a 4-4-2 or 4-2-3-1 and the whites are in a 4-2-3-1 or 4-4-2 with diamond.

The red goalkeeper starts the game and the red team build up play and try to score. If they lose the ball, the aim is to get it back very quickly again in the same grid where they lost it.

Once they win the ball back again, they must finish their attack within 8 seconds if they win the ball in zone 2 or 4-6 seconds if they win the ball in zone 1. If the white team passes into the safe zone they get 1 point and if they score a goal they get 2 points.

Rules

1. The same rules as the previous drill.
2. The red players can play in the safe zone when in possession, but the whites are not allowed.
3. When the white team have possession, they can play in the red safe zone. The reds are allowed once the ball has been played in there.

Coaching Points

1. Anticipation and fast decision making is needed to finish the attack quickly once the ball is won back.
2. The focus is again on a quick transition to defence by pressing the opponent in the same area the ball is lost.

GOAL ANALYSIS

Winning the Ball & One-Two Combination High Up the Pitch

09-Sep-2009: World Cup 2010 Qualifying

Spain 3-0 Estonia (1st Goal): Fabregas - Assist: Silva

Spain in a 4-3-3

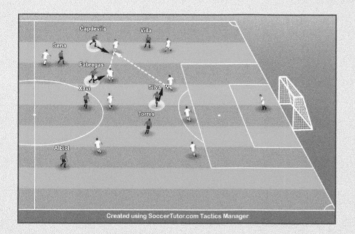

Spain press in the high zone. Estonia's centre back has the ball and Silva closes him down.

He passes to the right midfielder and Capdevila moves to press him.

The right midfielder passes inside to the centre midfielder and Fabregas recognises the situation. With good anticipation, Fabregas presses and wins the ball.

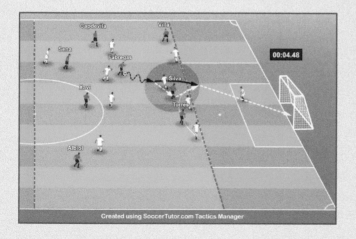

Fabregas dribbles forward and now has 4 opposition defenders and 3 teammates in front of him (4 v 4 situation).

He dribbles with the ball to draw a defender to him and when this happens, he plays a 1-2 combination with Silva into the space in behind and at the correct angle.

Fabregas scores with an excellent first time finish.

The attack took 4.48 seconds.

SESSION FOR THIS TOPIC *(5 Practices)*

1. One-Two Combinations with Passive Pressing

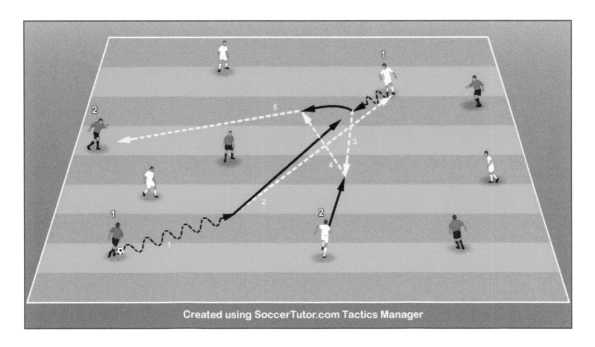

Created using SoccerTutor.com Tactics Manager

Objective

To develop running with the ball, pressing and one-two combinations.

Description

In an area 25 x 25 yards we have 2 teams of 5 players.

The reds start in possession. 1 red player dribbles with the ball, passes to an opponent and then runs across to apply passive defending to them.

The white player then dribbles forward up to the red defender and another teammate comes to support him to play a one-two combination.

The white player then passes to a red opponent and the practice continues in the same way.

Coaching Points

1. The first touch needs to be of high quality, allowing the player to immediately play a 1-2 combination.
2. The angle of the support player is key and should be monitored.
3. The weight, angle and accuracy of the first pass is important so the second pass in the 1-2 combination can easily be played first time and into the space and in front of the first player to run onto.
4. The pressing should be done at a high pace, as it represents a centre back closing the ball down at the edge of the penalty area.

PROGRESSION

2. One-Two Combinations in Direction of Play with Passive Pressing

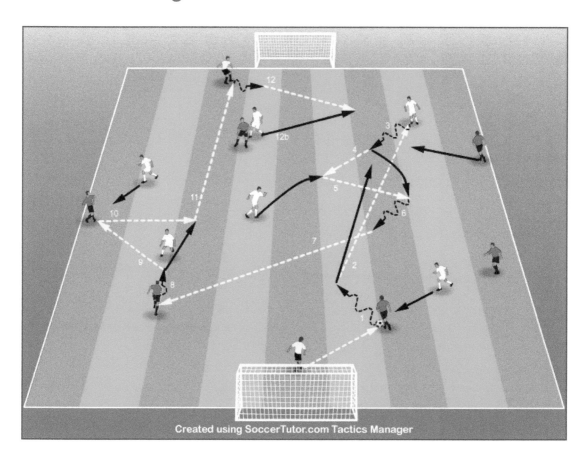

Created using SoccerTutor.com Tactics Manager

Description

In an area 35 x 25 yards we have the same practice as the previous one, but now we have 2 full sized goals.

The objectives are the same, but now the teams work in the direction of play as it is more realistic to represent a game situation.

Variation *(as shown in diagram)*

We can bring in 2 goalkeepers into the goals and after a one-two, the player must pass to the opposition goalkeeper and the practice continues with the goalkeeper rolling the ball out (or passing) to a teammate.

PROGRESSION
3. Dribbling, One-Two Combinations & Finishing Practice

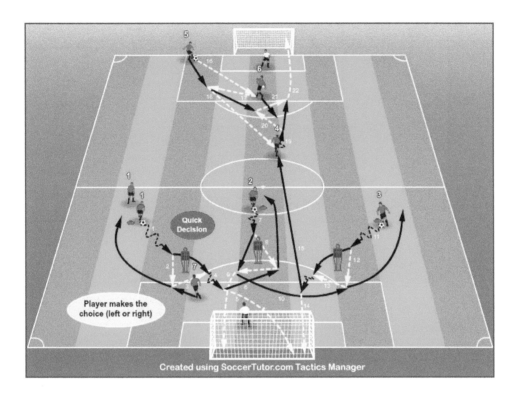

Created using SoccerTutor.com Tactics Manager

Objective

To develop support play for one-two combinations and finishing inside the penalty area.

Description

On a full pitch we have a minimum of 8 outfield players (can use many more), 2 goalkeepers and 3 mannequins.

Player 1 dribbles up to the mannequin. Player 7 chooses which side to provide support and player 1 plays a 1-2 combination with player 7 and then shoots at goal. Immediately after, player 2 dribbles up to the mannequin and player 1 plays the support role (1-2 and player 2 shoots on goal). Player 3 then dribbles up to the mannequin and player 2 now runs across to provide support (1-2 and player 3 shoots).

Player 3 (after shooting) runs up to the other half of the pitch into position 4. The play in the other half of the pitch starts with player 5 who plays a 1-2 combination with player 6 and passes to position 4. Player 6 turns and closes down player 4 (passive defending) who dribbles with the ball and player 5 moves to support player 4 for another 1-2 combination. After the 1-2 round the passive defender (player 6) player 4 shoots on goal.

Each player then moves to the next position (1 to 2, 2 to 3 etc) and the practice continues the same way.

257

PROGRESSION

4. Winning the Ball & One-Two Combinations in an 8 v 8 (+2) Small Sided Game

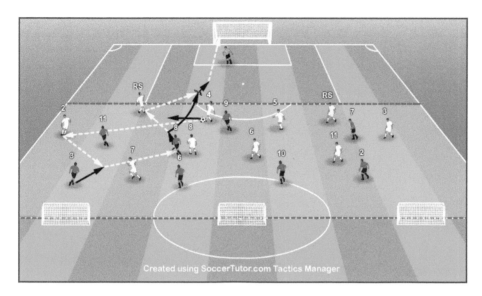

Objective

We work on using one-two combinations to get in behind the defensive line and finishing within a small sided game.

Description

Using half a pitch we create a zone between the halfway line and the edge of the penalty area. We put 3 mini goals on the halfway line and we have a full sized goal with a goalkeeper at the other end. Within the zone we have an 8v8 situation with 2 yellow support players who play only with the reds in possession. The reds are in a 2-3-3 formation from the 4-3-3 (2 FB, 3 MF & 3 AT) and the white team are in a 4-4 formation.

The game starts with the white goalkeeper and the white team try to score in the mini goals. The red team press within the zone and if they win the ball, the objective is to make a quick transition to attack and complete a counter attack within 6 seconds.

This 6 second time limit forces the white team to make a quick transition to defence and press the ball immediately. When this happens, the 2 yellow support players (or any other red player) move to provide support to the ball carrier who looks to play a 1-2 combination to break through pressure and play in behind the defensive line.

The reds try to move into the end zone and score. The whites are not allowed to enter the end zone.

Rules

1. The white team get 1 point if they score in either of the side mini goals & 2 points if they score in the middle one.
2. The red team get 1 point if they score a goal within 6 seconds and 2 points if this happens after a 1-2 combination.
3. All players play with unlimited touches.

PROGRESSION
5. Winning the Ball & One-Two Combinations in a 9 v 9 Small Sided Game

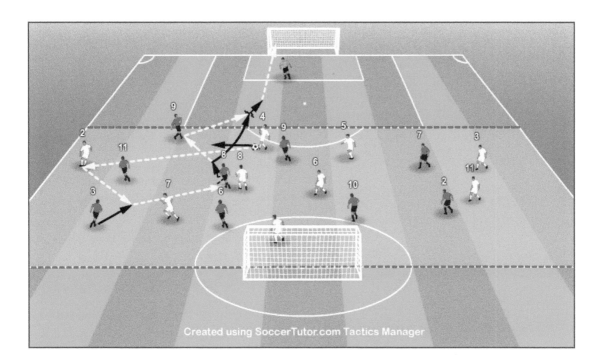

Created using SoccerTutor.com Tactics Manager

Description

In this progression we remove the 3 mini goals and replace them with a full sized goal. We remove the 2 support players and have 2 goalkeepers instead.

We play an 8v8 game with the same formations and objectives for both teams.

Progression

When the ball goes into the end zone all players from both teams are free to go in there to attack/defend.

Coaching Points

1. The positioning near the edge of the penalty area and angle of the support play (correct body shape) for the one-two combination is very important.

2. The weight, angle and accuracy of the first pass is important so the second pass in the 1-2 combination can easily be played first time and into the space in behind the defensive line.

3. The players should show good anticipation, decision making, quick and quality finishing.

GOAL ANALYSIS

Pressing High Up the Pitch: Transition from Defence to Attack (1)

29-Mar-2011: European Championship 2012 Qualifying

Lithuania 1-3 Spain (1st Goal): Xavi - Assist: Villa

Spain in a 4-3-3 vs Lithuania in a 4-4-2

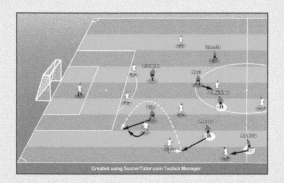

Spain are defending in the high zone and Alonso presses the opposition's right back.

The right back tries to play a long pass and the ball deflects off Alonso and goes behind the right centre back and towards David Villa.

Villa is faster than the centre back and takes possession of the ball.

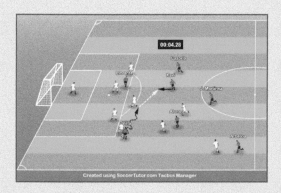

Villa dribbles inside and passes inside to Xavi.

Cazorla is also coming up from behind to support Villa and Llorente is in the penalty area.

There is a 4 v 4 situation.

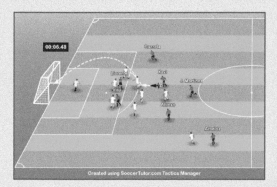

Xavi moves forward and a defender closes him down.

Xavi shoots and the ball hits the defender and takes a huge looping deflection and lobs the goalkeeper into the net.

The attack took 6.48 seconds.

SESSION FOR THIS TOPIC *(3 Practices)*

1. Quick Transition to Attack / Defence Dynamic 9 v 9 Possession Game

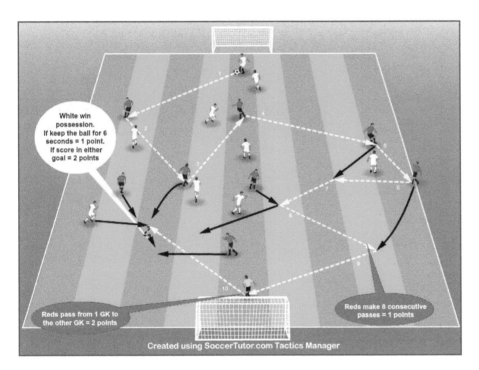

White win possession.
If keep the ball for 6 seconds = 1 point.
If score in either goal = 2 points

Reds pass from 1 GK to the other GK = 2 points

Reds make 8 consecutive passes = 1 points

Created using SoccerTutor.com Tactics Manager

Objective

To develop possession play with a focus on the quick transition from attack to defence and defence to attack.

Description

In an area 60 x 40 yards we play a 9v9 game. The objective for the red team (in a 3-2-3 formation) is to keep possession and pass the ball from one goal to the other goal (through the goalkeepers). They get 1 point when they complete 8 passes and 2 points when they successfully switch the ball from one goalkeeper to another.

The defending team (whites) try to win the ball. If they do, they score 1 point for keeping possession for 6 seconds and 2 points for scoring a goal.

This means that when the red team lose the ball they must make a quick transition to defence. They should press the ball carrier and the teammates around him very quickly at a high intensity. If the red team win the ball back within 4-6 seconds of losing it they score 3 points.

Different Rules

1. All players have unlimited touches.
2. The white players have unlimited touches, the reds and the goalkeepers are limited to 2 or 3 touches.
3. The white players have unlimited touches, the reds have 2 touches and the goalkeepers have 1 touch.

261

PROGRESSION
2. High Press & Counter Attack in a 9 v 7 (+4) Small Sided Game

Objective

We work on pressing high and preventing forward passes (especially out wide) with quick counter attacking play.

Description

Using the same size area, the red team have 8 players outfield players inside in a 2-3-3 (from 4-3-3) and the white team have 6 players inside in a 4-2 formation and 4 outside (4-4-2 formation). We have an 9 v 7 (+4) situation.

The game starts with the white goalkeeper and when he passes the ball, the red team start a high press with the objective to block passes from inside players to the outside players and win the ball.

If the reds win the ball they must finish their counter attack within 6 seconds. After the attack is finished, start again from the white goalkeeper.

Different Rules

1. All players have unlimited touches.
2. White inside players have unlimited touches, whites outside have 2 touches and the red players have 2-3 touches.
3. White inside players have unlimited touches, whites outside have 1 touch and the red players have 2-3 touches.
4. When a white inside player passes successfully to a white outside player the white team score 1 point.
5. If the white team score a goal they get 2 points.
6. The outside players are not allowed to score goals.

PROGRESSION
3. High Press & Counter Attacking in a Position Specific Game

Description

Using a full pitch we put a full sized goal without a goalkeeper 5 yards in front of the penalty area as shown. We also mark out 2 zones (the small one is 10 yards long) and another which shows the high zone for the red team to press (defend).

The red team are in a 4-3-3 formation with a V in the middle and the white team use a 4-4-2.

We play a normal free game starting with the white goalkeeper. If the reds score they get 1 point and if they score in the transition phase within 6 seconds of winning the ball they get 2 points.

If the white team successfully pass in behind the back of the red team's defence (into the small zone) they get 1 point and if they score a goal they get 2 points.

The goal without a goalkeeper forces the red team to make their transition from attack to defence much more quickly. They should do this by performing a quick high press on the ball carrier and the area around him.

Coaching Points

1. There needs to be good defensive cooperation between the midfielders & attackers to press in the high zone.
2. As soon as a red player wins the ball, players should be making runs in behind the defensive line. This is so a quick pass can be made and the attack can be finished within 6 seconds.
3. Collective pressing, anticipation, quick decision making and good combination play are the key elements.

GOAL ANALYSIS

Pressing High Up the Pitch: Transition from Defence to Attack (2)

03-Sep-2010: European Championship 2012 Qualifying

Liechtenstein 0-4 Spain (4th Goal): Silva - Assist: Busquets

Spain in a 4-4-2 vs Liechtenstein in a 4-2-3-1

The goalkeeper has passed the ball out to his right back.

Villa presses the right back high up on the flank and does not leave him space or the opportunity to dribble or pass the ball.

The Liechtenstein right back tries to pass forward but Villa blocks the ball which rebounds towards the byline.

Villa runs forward to press the right back again.

The other players close in on the ball zone and eliminate the passing options.

The right back makes a poor pass and Busquets gets to the ball faster than his direct opponent and wins possession of the ball.

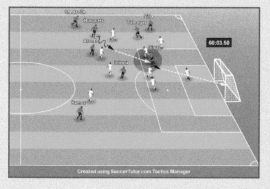

Spain now move into a transition to attack.

Busquets dribbles the ball inside and at the correct time passes into the box to Silva who has moved into a centre forward's position.

Silva takes an excellent directional first touch and with his second touch scores the goal.

This attack only took 3.5 seconds.

SESSION FOR THIS TOPIC *(5 Practices)*

1. Continuous Transition to Defence & then Transition to Attack in an 8 v 8 Dynamic Game

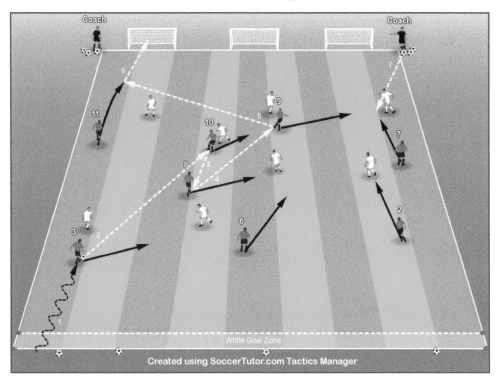

Created using SoccerTutor.com Tactics Manager

Objective

We work on attacking play with the focus on the transitions from defence to attack and attack to defence.

Description

In an area 60 x 40 yards we put 3 mini goals at one end and we have a goal line at the other. We play 8v8 (reds in a 2-4-2 / whites in a 4-4 formation). There are 2 coaches/players on the outside with lots of footballs.

Scenario 1: One red player dribbles the ball from the goal line and the first objective for the red team is to try and score in one of the 3 mini goals (1 point for either side goal & 2 points for the middle one). Once their attack is finished, the coach then immediately passes a new ball to the white team. The reds second objective is to then make a quick transition to defence, win the ball and attack for a second time (transition to attack).

The whites aim to score by dribbling (or passing & receiving) through the end goal line to score 2 points. When the second attack is finished another red player gets a new ball from the goal line and the drill continues in the same way.

Scenario 2: The red team continuously defend. A coach passes to a white player and the red team apply a high press trying to win the ball and then counter attack. When the red attack is finished, the other coach passes a new ball to another white player and the reds must switch the point of their defence and apply a new high press, win the ball and launch a new counter attack (at pace).

PROGRESSION
2. High Intensity 8 v 8 Pressing Game with Empty Goals

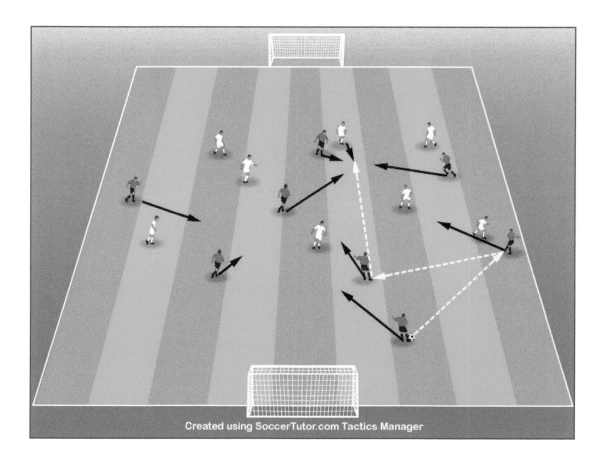

Created using SoccerTutor.com Tactics Manager

Objective

We focus on the transition from attack to defence which has to be done extremely quickly (pressing the ball carrier immediately) as there are no goalkeepers in the goals.

Description

In the same area (60 x 40 yards) we now have 2 full sized goals without goalkeepers. Both teams are either in a 3-2-3 or 2-4-2 formation. This small sided game should include pressing at a very high intensity. The players play a normal game, but the focus is on when a team loses possession.

When the ball is lost, the players should close the ball carrier down very quickly and not allow him the opportunity to shoot or pass to a teammate in a better position.

The 2 empty goals help a lot when training this situation. In this small sided game, the transition from defence to attack and attack to defence is continuous. When a team's attack is finished (score a goal or the ball goes out of play) the game continues immediately with the other team in possession.

SPAIN Attacking Sessions

PROGRESSION

3. Continuous Transition to Defence / Attack in an 8 v 8 Small Sided Game

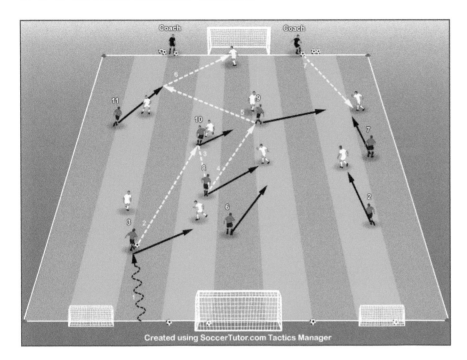

Created using SoccerTutor.com Tactics Manager

Objective

The continuous nature of this drill helps the players to make quick transitions from defence to attack and attack to defence.

Description

This practice combines the 2 previous drills into one in an area 60 x 40 yards. The red team are in a 2-3-3 formation and the white team are in a 4-4 formation. The red team shoot in the full sized goal with the goalkeeper and the white team shoot in the 3 goals without goalkeepers.

Part 1: The game starts with one red player (3) who dribbles the ball from the end line. The red team attack and once their attack is finished (a goal is scored or the ball goes out of play) the coach immediately passes a new ball to the white team and the reds must make a quick transition from attack to defence. They apply pressure high up to win the ball back as quickly as possible and then counter attack.

When this new red attack is finished, another red player must return back and get a new ball from the end line, starting a new attack by dribbling the ball forwards. If the white team attack and score a goal or the ball goes out of play, the coach immediately passes a new ball to the white team. The red team press high again to win the ball and launch another counter attack.

Part 2: We change the game slightly so the red team are continuously working on the transition from defence to attack. The game starts with a coach passing to the white team. The red team apply pressure high up to win the ball as quickly as possible and then counter attack.

When a red team's attack is finished, the other coach immediately passes a new ball into another white player and the red team must make a quick transition from attack to defence, again pressing high up to win the ball as quickly as possible and counter attack again. The game continues this way and works on a continuous loop (even if the whites score).

SPAIN Attacking Sessions

PROGRESSION

4. Continuous Dynamic 9 v 9 Transition Game with Shooting Zone

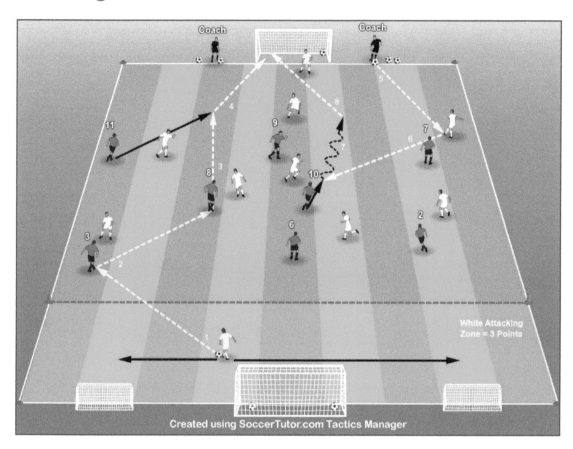

Description

We use the same area again (60 x 40 yards) and make 2 changes to the previous practice. A 15 x 40 yard zone is created at the end with 3 goals and a goalkeeper is added who defends all 3.

White team: When they complete 4 passes they get 1 point, if they pass to the red goalkeeper they get 2 points (goalkeeper passes to red team after receiving) and if they move the ball into the end zone they get 3 points. Scoring in either of the 2 mini goals gets 4 points and scoring in the middle goal gets 5 points.

Red team: If they win the ball they get 1 point, if they score in the goal they get 2 points and if they score within 6 seconds of winning the ball they get 3 points. The coach keeps passing new balls into the white team immediately after an attack is finished to keep the drill continuous.

Coaching Points

1. There needs to be good defensive cooperation between the midfielders & attackers to press in the high zone.
2. Good concentration and anticipation is needed to react quickly for a transition to defence or attack.

PROGRESSION
5. Winning Possession High Up the Pitch in an 11 v 11 Transition Game

Description

We now work on the same ideas as all the previous drills in the session on a full pitch with an 11v11 game. The red team are in a 4-3-3 with a V in the middle and the white team are in 4-4-2 with a bowl.

The game starts with the red goalkeeper and the red team try to attack and score (red players are limited to 2-3 touches. The focus of this practice is when/if they lose the ball.

If the white team win the ball and keep possession for 6-8 seconds or complete 4-6 passes they get 1 point. If the whites move the ball into the end zone they get 2 points and if they score a goal they get 3 points.

All these rules force the red team to defend by pressing in the high zone (quick transition from attack). The reds get 1 point for a normal goal and 2 points if they score within 6 seconds of winning the ball back from the opposition.

The coach passes a new ball to the white team immediately after an attack is finished or the ball goes out of play which makes both teams react quickly to a transition to defence (or attack) and keeps the game continuous.

Coaching Points

1. There needs to be good defensive cooperation between the midfielders & attackers to press in the high zone.
2. Good concentration and anticipation is needed to react quickly for a transition to defence or attack.

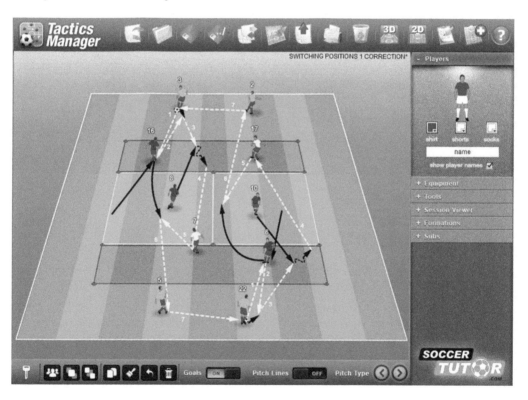

Lightning Source UK Ltd.
Milton Keynes UK
UKHW051213190622
404623UK00003B/37